Tales from the Trips

Tales from the Trips

How I Grew To Be A Father

Robert J. Bresky Jr.

iUniverse, Inc.
Bloomington

Tales From The Trips
How I Grew To Be A Father

iUniverse books may be ordered through booksellers or by contacting:

iUniverse
1663 Liberty Drive
Bloomington, IN 47403
www.iuniverse.com
1-800-Authors (1-800-288-4677)

ISBN: 978-1-4620-1963-2 (sc)
ISBN: 978-1-4620-1964-9 (ebk)

Printed in the United States of America

iUniverse rev. date: 07/21/2011

CONTENTS

Thanks to my parents, Robert and Lucille Sr.; my wife, Carol; my son, Christopher; my daughter, Rachel; my son-in-law, Phil and grandson, Sampson;my sisters, Lucille and Cynthia; and brothers, Douglas, Paul, Wayne, and Charles. For friends, new and old, I met on my travels.

Illustrations

Preface

Different places, different faces, and different spaces have shaped my life since childhood. I was born in Brooklyn, New York, raised in the New Jersey suburbs, and schooled in Philadelphia, Pennsylvania; Washington, DC; Seattle, Washington; Anchorage, Alaska; and Portland, Oregon. Besides moving to new places to meet family and job responsibilities, leisure travel has also been a constant in my life. My father's international stamp collection, business, and vacation travel have inspired me to explore North American, Caribbean, and European destinations. I wrote this book to educate, entertain, and inspire others about traveling and to share stories that framed important milestones in my life history.

The book's primary sources include personal observations and photographs, written notes, a diary, and journals. I also used published information from tourist bureaus, chambers of commerce, state and federal agencies, and websites. Lonely Planet, Frommer's, and Moon tour books provided guidance on lodging, tours, and restaurants. National Geographic, Discovery Channel, and public television programs identified sites to see and how and when to see them.

My father instilled in me a joy for airline travel by taking me on my first plane trip to Pittsburgh, Pennsylvania. John Steinbeck's *Travels with Charley* and William Least Heat-Moon's *Blue Highways* inspired me to take road trips in America. Mark Twain's *The Innocents Abroad* opened my eyes to foreign travel. Authors like John McPhee and John Muir shaped what I looked at, while Garrison Keillor and Stephen Colbert helped me use comedy in my storytelling. Like the song titles that introduce most of its chapters, Tales From the Trips doesn't follow one lyrical style, tempo or rhythm. The operatic Bicycle Race through

Europe has classical overtones while North to Alaska conjures up country songs about trophy salmon and grizzly bears. The reggae song No Woman, No Cry and soft rock song Mexico harken to secluded beaches and underground rivers. Rocky Mountain Way rock and rolls rafters on Colorado's exciting white water rapids. Poetic reflections in California Scheming echo the environmental and conservation ethics of a 1960's folk song. In short, Tales From the Trips is a travel memoir that is emotionally charged like any good song.

Chapter One

"Bicycle Race"

The highlight of my college junior year was a July–August 1972 bicycle tour of Western Europe. For two months, I cycled to and from American Youth Hostels in seven countries: England, France, Germany, Austria, Italy, Switzerland, and the Netherlands. My father strongly encouraged me to take the trip to broaden my education. But I always suspected his real motive was to separate me from my then steady girlfriend, Carol, of whom he disapproved. He gave me a bound diary to record the details. His dating advice was to keep playing the field. He wanted me to be a player.

My fellow travelers included one of my fraternity brothers, Tom, and strangers from all over the United States. Our tour leader was picked for his cycling experience, not for his interpersonal or navigational skills. A fit female accounting major from New York, Donna, and a buff Southern Californian surfer dude, Roger, bonded through their athletic abilities. A freckled-faced tomboy from Brown University, Kathy, was liked by everybody for her ability to listen and laugh. She fell in love with an intelligent teacher, Mark, who had strong conservative views and leadership qualities. A model from Georgia, Jackie, and a gay Jew from New York, Alan, rounded out our group, which reminded me of a cast from a reality television show.

Our amazing race departed from JFK Airport on a red-eye flight to London's Heathrow Airport. We arrived in London at 9:00 a.m., after losing five hours with time changes. We used buses and the underground to see Buckingham Palace's changing of the guards, Trafalgar Square, and the National Gallery. After dinner at our youth hostel, the group enjoyed warm pints of bitter at Gunner's Pub before returning to the hostel for sleep.

Changing of the Guard

The second day in London, we assembled our bikes, which were stored at the Holland House Youth Hostel, and rode them to Westminster Abbey, Madame Tussauds Wax Museum, and Regent's Park. That night, three of us saw the play *Lloyd George Knew My Father*. The next day, I separated from the group to meet my high school sweetheart, Beth, who dumped me my high school senior year. Beth was in college to be an interior designer and was studying art in London that summer. We toured the Tower of London and attended an evening performance of *The Tempest* under the stars at Regent's Park. We caught each other up on our lives since our breakup and kissed good night. I wondered if coincidence drew us together or if my father had conspired to make this chance encounter happen. I never asked. He never said.

After three days in London, our tour group and bicycles took a train from the Waterloo Station to Sevenoaks and cycled to Crockham Hill in the English countryside. The next day, we cycled thirty-five miles to Goudhurst, where we stayed at the Twysden Manor Youth Hostel, which closed in 1980. That was followed by a twenty-four-mile cycle to Blackboys Hostel, a wooden lodge with nine bunk beds per room, set on an acre of ancient woodland. The name of the hostel alluded to its policy of welcoming all travelers regardless of race, color, or religion. Most youth hostels we stayed in opened at 5:00 p.m. and closed at 10:00 a.m., offering inexpensive dinners and breakfasts.

Our next bicycle ride was to Alfriston, a distance of twenty miles. We celebrated July 4, Independence Day, at Ye Olde Smuggler's Pub. On July 5, three of us cycled to Seaford, where we washed clothes and ate lunch, overlooking scenic white cliffs.

On our last day in England, we biked eight miles to New Haven, where we boarded the ferry to Dieppe, France. It took three and a half hours to cross the English Channel. From there, we hopped on a train to Paris and checked in for a three-night stay at an elementary school turned hostel for the summer.

The architecture and landscaping in the City of Lights reminded me of Washington DC, a Frenchman-designed (Pierre L'Enfant) city I first visited during a college field trip. Captured by its romantic beauty, I started having feelings for Jackie.

While in Paris, we used public transportation to reach popular tourist sites, such as the Notre Dame Cathedral, the Louvre, and the Eiffel Tower. Most nights, we dined in the Latin Quarter and returned to the hostel to sleep. To my embarrassment, I discovered that wearing shorts in Paris was a fashion faux pas. I also learned that street musicians played everywhere, even in the metro subway stations. Sounds of bongo drums, guitars, and harmonicas echoed throughout the cavernous station platforms and tunnels.

From our Paris hostel, we cycled to Gare de Lyon, where we saw the famous paintings of *Mona Lisa* and the *Whistler's Mother* and a sculpture of Venus, the Roman goddess of love and beauty. After dinner, we rode the night train to Bern, Switzerland. Playing hearts and drinking wine helped make the eight-and-a-half hour trip a merry one.

Despite the dreary weather, Bern shone like a star radiating the brightness of the Swiss Alps. Unfortunately, a meager continental breakfast of rolls and butter failed to dazzle us like the scenery. Dreaming on the train, I envisioned a heartier American fare like pancakes, bacon, and scrambled eggs. After breakfast, we shopped and I bought a Swiss clock. We had to tolerate the smells and dirt from the road until 8:30 p.m., when the hostel turned on hot water showers for seventy-five minutes.

The next day, we picked up our bicycles at the Bern train station and cycled twenty rainy miles to Thun. There, we ate lunch and went sightseeing in this beautiful, busy, and clean city. We toured Thun Castle and walked along the narrow city streets lined with bakeries and watch and cuckoo clock stores. In the afternoon, we cycled to our hostel in Faulensee, which overlooked the Swiss Alps and a lake. We went to sleep hungry, because the hostel lacked hot water and cooking facilities.

A substantial breakfast of scrambled and hard-boiled eggs and delicious French bread greeted us the next morning. Our stomachs full, we cycled to Interlaken, located between Tuhn and Brienz lakes. We hopped on a train to Grindelwald. Our train window framed gorgeous waterfalls and mountain glaciers as we moved through the Grindelwald Valley. The Grindelwald hostel was in a great-looking Swiss chalet perched above the valley, but it required quite a hike to reach. Dinner tasted good and the hostel had hot water. However, in my sleeping bag, I felt like a squished roll of insulation wedged between two-by-fours that passed as our attic bed.

I woke up sick either from food poisoning or from the less-than-healthy sleeping accommodations. I stayed in bed until my headache and stomachache abated. Then I had breakfast and took a ski lift to Bort, halfway up a 1,600-foot mountain. Three of us walked down, taking pictures of the mountains and wild flowers. The rest of the group hiked further to a nearby glacier.

The next day, six of us explored Oberglacier. We took a chairlift halfway up a mountain and hiked to the start of the greenish-blue glacier. We climbed twelve ladders of varying lengths and angles until we reached the summit. Young and unafraid of icy steps or slick railings, I felt free and oblivious to any safety concerns.

After returning from our hike and climb, we cycled ten miles to our lakeside hostel in Brienz, where we slept. After riding the rails to Giswil, we cycled twenty miles through a steady mist to Stans, where we stopped for lunch. Then we pedaled to Beckenreid, where we caught the ferry to Gersau. The hostel at Gersau had spacious bunk beds, hot showers, and good food. After a dinner of veal cutlets and potatoes, three of us biked into town, where we drank beer and listened to "The Night They Drove Old Dixie Down" in German.

The next day, three of us cycled to a lake to swim. The glacial-fed water was about forty-two degrees Fahrenheit, so we spent more time sunbathing than swimming. After a scrumptious dinner of veal and potatoes, we drank beer until bedtime.

The next morning, the tour group cycled to Vitznau to relax at the beach. We enjoyed music, rafts, paddleboards, and a picnic lunch, complete with chocolate. Part of the group took the ferry to Lucerne, while three others and I sweated eighteen miles to get there on bikes. From Lucerne, it was a fourteen-hour train ride to Roma, Italy. One of our female cyclists, longing to see her boyfriend, left the tour to return home.

Rome bustled with activity when we arrived at 10:00 a.m. We took a bus to our hostel because there were no underground trains like in England and France. Since our hostel didn't open until 4:00 p.m., we swam in an Olympic-sized pool. Our hearty appetites enjoyed a two-dollar dinner of fruit salad, custard, lasagna, meatballs, lima beans, squid salad, and wine. The meal was the best of the trip.

Because of the heat, time constraints, crazy drivers, and the availability of inexpensive public transportation, we did not cycle in Italy. Rather, we took buses or boats wherever we needed to go. One bus took us to the Vatican Museum and Sistine Chapel. I was overwhelmed by the detail and grandeur of Michelangelo's ceiling art. The sight inspired me to take a history of art class when I returned to Penn for my senior year.

After examining the human body from afar, it was off to the Lido (beach) to see female bodies in the flesh swimming in the Mediterranean Sea. Only words as salty as the water could describe the Italian women in their tight-fitting and microscopic swimwear.

The next day, we walked around the Coloseum ruins, the Forum, and the Pantheon. Like rats escaping the scorching heat, we headed underground to tunnels (the Catacombs), where Christians hid from Roman persecution. As a Christian, I doubt I would have the courage to die for my faith. I hope I never have to make that choice.

After dinner, two of us went to see the opera *Aida*, staged at the Roman baths. In contrast to German opera, which underplayed the voice, Italian opera emphasized the vocal talents of its actors.

From Rome, we took a train to Florence (Firenze). The ride seemed longer than three and a half hours because of the boring and brown scenery. We took a bus to the hostel, located in a stately villa formerly owned by Mussolini's mistress. The Spanish-style hostel was set in the woods and was fronted by a large ornate fountain. To celebrate Kathy's birthday, we made peach shortcake for dessert.

Florence was a shopper's paradise. I found good deals on cashmere sweaters and leather sandals at the Mercato Centrale (central market). Two of us walked to the Ponte Vecchio, a covered bridge spanning the Arno River. Unlike the spartan-covered bridges in America, this bridge was filled with stores like a mall. From there, we headed to the Duomo and saw the Cathedral of Santa Maria del Fiore, Giatto's Tower, and the Baptistery. From there, we walked to Pitti Palace and enjoyed the lovely landscaped grounds. The final stop before dinner was the Piazzle de Michelangelo and its beautiful view of Florence.

After dinner, Roger and I compared our feelings for the sweet-talking Jackie, while we drank Red Garter beers and listened to mediocre music. We lost track of the time and returned to the hostel after it closed. As a result, we spent the night on the grass with two Canadian drinking buddies, who met the same fate.

Sleep deprived after outdoor camping, I drank lots of coffee before another day of sightseeing. I slowly walked to the Academy Gallery to see *David*, the towering Michelangelo sculpture. Feeling insignificant next to such grand art, I climbed the bell tower in Duomo Square to get a different perspective. Chills ran down my spine as I entered the Cathedral of Santa Maria del Fiore and saw two pietas by Michelangelo. More personal and intimate than the Sistine Chapel, I wept at the marble statues of a grieving mother holding the lifeless body of her only son.

Chapters in the Bible's Old Testament came to life in the bronze-cast and gold-painted Ghiberti doors. Seeing these Renaissance doors was like reading an illustrated version of the Bible with three-dimensional glasses. To further immerse myself in the Renaissance masters, I entered the Uffizi Gallery to gaze upon the genius of Raphael, Rubens, Van Dyck, Rembrandt, and Fiorentino.

From the marble and bronze of Florence, we headed to Venice, known for its blown glass. The train ride lasted three hours and was punctuated by tunnels and dull vistas. As the train crossed a bridge into Venice, I saw oil refineries like the ones seen from the Goethals Bridge leading to Staten Island, New York. Modern industrial development contrasted with the preindustrial grandeur of the city's waterfront residential and business districts.

A motorized boat delivered our group to a hostel located on one of Venice's famous canals. The weather was hot and sunny, so we cooled off in the Adriatic. The water was calm, warm, and salty. Several group members built a huge sand castle (early grotesque architectural style) that attracted a crowd. We met a local Venetian named Enrico, who taught us some conversational Italian. After doing laundry, we boated to Murano Island to see a glass-blowing demonstration. We gawked at the expensive, beautiful, and ornate chandeliers; shimmering ashtrays; and colorful clowns. Returning to San Marco, Venice's town square, we listened to a Venetian band play to an audience of hundreds of pigeons. Then we toured the Peggy Guggenheim Museum, where the oldest art was from the twentieth rather than the fifteenth century. After a seafood dinner, three group members got sick while riding the train to Vienna, Austria.

We arrived at a clean and modern train station, exchanged money, and ate breakfast. Then we rode the bus to our youth hostel located on the outskirts of town. The hostel set on spacious grounds was modern, inexpensive, and clean, with extended curfews. Jackie and I went to the Spanish Riding School to see the Lippizan horses and then to the Hopsburg Palace. Hand in hand, we walked by St. Stephens Cathedral and saw the parliament and St. Maria Theresa Gardens. Back at the hostel, we enjoyed running, Keep Away, and catch.

Day thirty-two, halfway through our trip, Jackie and I decided to explore St. Stephen's Church. The church's original roof was destroyed during World War II and replaced with mosaic tile. We climbed up to the bell towers for a bird's-eye view. After our one-dollar lunch of stuffed pepper, rice, and pudding, we strolled along the green and murky Danube River. Then we sauntered to Schonbrunn Palace, where we explored the large gardens, maze, obelisk, zoo, and aquarium. After a pork chop dinner, Donna, Kathy, Roger, and I heard the Berliner Oktett perform works by Schubert at the Palace Ausberg.

Sunday, day thirty-four, Jackie and I tried to tour the Vienna porcelain factory, but it was closed. We walked around the Prater (amusement park) instead. The park had the largest and slowest Ferris wheel I had ever seen and also a unique attraction called the Rent-A-Train Set. As a young boy, I loved my Lionel train set and spent many hours moving engines and railcars through rural and urban settings.

After a very filling lunch of traditional Austrian food (Weiner schnitzel) Hungarian goulash, dumplings, and apple strudel), we toured the inside of Schonbrunn Palace. Most impressive was the $6-million room with gold, porcelain, rococo, and baroque details. We capped off the day dancing to a live band at the Tenne discotheque.

Day thirty-five, the tour group caught a midmorning train to Salzburg, arriving early afternoon. The warden at the Salzburg hostel was nicknamed "the Fuhrer" because he maintained very strict curfews and economized by using newspaper in the toilets. The beds lacked mattresses, so we slept on boards. As a result, we were early risers.

Day thirty-six, we saw Hitler's summer home called Berchetesgaden. Unfortunately, my fraternity brother forgot his passport and had to return to the hostel when we reached the German border. From the bus stop, it was an hour's hike to Konigssee Lake. We toured the lake by boat, listening to a horn concerto, and saw Hitler's tearoom and castle, where scenes from the *Sound of Music* movie were filmed. At night, we watched Vienna's Marionette Theater perform *Magic Flute*. Nature and music fed my spirit while veal nourished my body.

Day thirty-seven, we cycled nine miles to Hallein to see its famous salt mine. It was crowded, with a four-and-a-half-hour waiting line. Rather than stand in the rain waiting, we hiked around the mine's entrance and down the mountain, stopping for a picnic lunch. Next, we cycled sixteen miles to Werfen in the pouring rain. Our reward for a muddy, tiring, and soggy day was a candlelit dinner in a castle. Despite lightning, thunder, and dreams of dungeon spirits, my weary body slept soundly.

My first mechanical problem occurred on the thirty-eigth day, when two bicycle spokes broke. Frustrated by an unsuccessful search for a repair shop, I cycled thirty-five miles on a crippled back tire. Arriving behind the rest of the group, the Zell am See hostel managers directed me to a bicycle repair shop, where I replaced the broken spokes. Penny-wise but pound foolish, I later regretted not buying a new tire rim. Riding with a bent rim was slow and tiring, not to mention dangerous.

Day thirty-nine marked the seventh straight day of rain. Reading and writing letters to Carol and my family lifted my spirits on a dreary day spent at the Zell am See hostel. I also wrote in my diary and read Irving Stone's novel *Passions of the Mind* about Sigmund Freud's life and career in western Europe.

Either inspired by the dirndls, knickers, and lederhosen worn by our hosts or just too lazy to wash his dirty clothes, Mark bought a lederhosen outfit and modeled it in front of a laughing and clapping audience. For those who cycled to the laundry to wash clothes, it did not have a happy ending. Neurotic Alan crashed his three-speed bike on a slick downhill mountain ride. His retelling of the harrowing crash and his rescue by two burly Austrian truckers kept us laughing all night. Clearly shaken by the accident, he took trains the rest of our trip.

I woke up the morning of the fortieth day dead tired because a loud Austrian folk band played during an all-night party. Wearily, I mounted my bike, with its wobbly back tire, and cycled thirty-five rainy miles to Kitzbuhel. Half of the cycling was climbing four thousand feet. After the grueling ascent, I appreciated the challenges faced by racers like Lance Armstrong in the Tour de France.

Wet, dirty, but exhilarated after a fast downhill from Pass Thun, we stopped for lunch and coasted downhill for the remainder of the trip. An Austrian family with two children owned the guesthouse (hostel) in Kitzbuhel. I shared a room, sink, comfortable beds, and closet with three other riders. After dinner, we partied at the local disco until past midnight, exchanging deep kisses and dirty dances with Jackie.

The sun woke us up on day forty-one, making its first morning appearance in over a week. Jackie, Kathy, and I cycled to town for lunch and watched an Austrian parade of marching bands, fire engines, and pretty girls. For dinner, I had asparagus, tapioca soup, smoked ham, and banana pastry. That night, the four of us sampled Bavarian food, drinks, and music and listened to six bands at Kitzbuhel's centennial celebration, which reminded me of an Oktoberfest.

The sun paid us another visit on day forty-two. We cycled twenty-five miles to Kufstein. Overlooking the town, the hostel was in an old stone mansion with an orange tile roof. If cycling up and down mountain passes to Zell am Zee was the most physical leg of our trip, then riding from Kitzbuhel to Kufstein was the most exciting and dangerous. Through high speed turns on gravel strewn roads, I glided on skinny tires without a helmet. Sylvan mountains, waterfalls, and gorges passed in a blur until I slowly coasted into town. We patronized the Wienerwald restaurant in Kufstein for both lunch and dinner since it had great-quality food at low prices. Besides good food, Kufstein's other claim to fame was its Kneissl downhill ski factory.

For the third consecutive morning, the sun greeted us as we awoke on day forty-three. We pedaled to Woergl, where we hailed a train to Innsbruck, host city for the 1964 and 1976 Winter Olympics. Innsbruck was a large city nestled between huge mountains. The hostel looked like an athlete's dream. The dormitory had eight Ping-Pong tables, a gymnasium, basketball courts, soccer nets, hot showers, and nice lounges. We celebrated Tom's birthday with a chocolate cake, complete with twenty-two candles.

After finishing William Roth's book entitled *Our Gang*, I started reading *The Ugly American*. I fell asleep and woke up to another beautiful sunny morning on day forty-four. I walked around and window-shopped for Kneissl and Fischer downhill boots and skis. Donna and I sat in the park to read after lunch. I then joined Tom for dinner at another Wienerwald restaurant. After banana splits, we listened to a Bavarian folk band. They played Austrian, Mexican, and other world music. Roger, who personified an ugly American, came home drunk again, mumbling about the big-breasted Austrian women he saw. He must have had some wild dreams that night, because he fell out of his bunk.

On day forty-five, we rode the rails to Mittenwald, Germany, where Jackie and I cycled thirteen miles to Garmisch-Partenkirchen. Pine and fir trees covered the lush green countryside. The hostel, about three kilometers outside of Garmisch, had good food, nice bedrooms, and hot showers. I eagerly read mail from Carol; a college roommate and fraternity brother; his girlfriend; Beth; and my maternal grandmother. The tour group played Frisbee, Ping-Pong, and pinball after dinner and listened to jukebox tunes. After finishing *The Ugly American*, I fell asleep to the Voice of America and Radio Luxembourg.

Sunshine accompanied us for the sixth consecutive day as three of us cycled into town for lunch makings. We then pedaled to the Garmisch Olympic Stadium and on to the gorge and caverns of Partnachklamm.

Crystal clear waterfalls ran through caves and small gorges. After spelunking, we hiked to a nearby hill, where we ate our picnic lunch. The hillside was to be the site of the 1940 Winter Olympics, which was cancelled due to World War II. Peaceful world competition lost out to guns and violence, resulting in huge losses of life. Purple Hearts and Congressional Medals of Honor replaced gold, silver, and bronze medals.

We cycled thirty miles in the hot sunshine from Garmisch to Weilheim, where we caught the train to Munchen (Munich), the capital of West Germany. Our group leader got a flat tire along the route but was able to fix it in time to catch the train.

Upon arriving in Munchen, we cycled to our hostel about a mile from the *banhof* (train station). After lunch, we walked to the site of the 1972 Summer Olympics, where several Israeli athletes were killed just weeks after we visited. We toured the cycling coliseum (velodrome) with its impressive wooden track. The modern glass roof on one building seemed to clash with the more natural surroundings of other athletic venues.

That night, Jackie and I met some Harvard freshmen at the Hofbrau House, where we listened to a band, watched a fist fight, and downed about three one-liter mugs of overflowing German beer. The waitress' ability to serve heavy trays of overflowing mugs without spilling dwarfed our ability to drink what she served.

On day forty-eight, we toured the Deutches Museum, which included exhibits on mining, submarines, physics, and astronomy. Then we cycled to the Nymphenburg Palace, Hunting Lodge, and Coach Museum, where Olympic equestrian events occurred.

Day forty-nine, we cycled twenty-two miles round-trip to and from the Dachau concentration camp. Sweating from the ninety-degree weather, I could not complain about the heat after learning how hot the camp's crematorium burned. The camp's museum and barracks conveyed the horror of the Holocaust better than books.

Day fifty, we took a four-hour train ride to Heidelburg, home of the Heidelburg Castle. Two of us toured the castle with a funny guide, who showed us its gigantic wine vat in the cellar, along with its glockenspiel box. The castle's Renaissance and baroque doors and windows were made from over eight types of wood.

Because of inclement weather, four group members took the train to Darmstadt while three others and I cycled thirty-one miles and met the rest of the group at the Darmstadt train station. My jeans were covered in mud and sand after the trip and so was my bicycle. I dried out on the train ride to Mainz. After picking up our mail, we cycled through a lovely park to reach our hostel on the Rhine River.

All of the group, except for one, cycled thirty-five miles to Oberwesel, stopping in Bingen for lunch. The last fifteen miles of our route took us along the Rhine, where castles seemed to appear as often as exits on the Garden State Parkway. Only, these "white castles" didn't sell burgers. We passed lots of river traffic, including barges, tugboats, and sightseeing boats. Our hostel had lousy food, but its balcony views of the Rhine and its Armed Forces Network radio broadcasts were great.

Day fifty-four brought a mixture of sun and rain showers. We headed to town for lunch and dinner, knowing the poor quality of the hostel food. Wine, Jaeger schnitzel (veal and mushrooms), and Schwein schnitzel were the favorably reviewed menu choices. Ice cream and dancing to the tunes of a female disc jockey followed.

Windy conditions made day fifty-five a challenge as we cycled twenty-five miles to Koblenz. Our tour leader got another flat tire along the way. Fortunately, we escaped the elements by taking a train from Koblenz to Bonn. We checked our bikes at the train station and rode a bus to a comfortable hostel in Ippendorf that served good food.

Jackie and I toured Bonn and met a young man from Edinburg. He led us to Beethoven's birthplace and residence. Not far away, a bridge connected Bonn to a town called Buhl. On the Bonn side of the bridge, a statute of a man bent over with britches at his ankles, exposed his shiny posterior towards Buhl. Our British guide explained that "Bonn residents angry at Buhl residents who refused to tax themselves to help pay for building the shared bridge, commissioned a statute that would forever show their disdain for the Scrooges from Buhl". The story engaged me like no economics lecture at Wharton could.

Day fifty-seven, we shipped our bikes to Arnhem, Germany and took a train to Cologne. From Cologne, we rode the rails to Arnhem to retrieve our cycles. I was disappointed to find that my back tire now had five broken spokes, probably due to riding on a bent rim. With the trip almost over, I rode trains for long distances and used my damaged bike for short trips.

Our Arnhem hostel was located in a beautiful park and included an all-you-can-eat breakfast. I bussed to the Hoge Veluwe National Park in Holland to see the Kroller-Muller Museum and its wonderful collection of almost three hundred Van Gogh paintings. The twenty-two-acre park was a beautiful setting for the museum, with its weeping willows, moors, sand dunes, and lakes. It was Holland's largest nature preserve and animal sanctuary.

Returning to Arnhem's train station, I took a train to Amersfoort, the Netherlands, where I cycled to a hostel for the night. Day fifty-nine, the group took the train to Amsterdam, our last stop before flying back to New York City. In Amsterdam, we toured the Rijksmuseum to see their famed Rembrandt collection. I bought a print of his *Night Watch* painting for my mother. That night, we stayed in a hostel about fifteen miles from Amsterdam. It was in a quaint country house with music playing in every room.

Our final touring day included a visit to the Heineken Brewery, which required arising early and getting in line by 8:00 a.m. A postcard I kept from the brewery visit showed that Heineken donated my admission fee to UNICEF, the United Nation's Children Fund. We waited another two hours before entering the brewery. After the tour, I bought Kathy and Mark a glass-enclosed brass clock for a wedding gift. The bride-to-be was an eighteen-year-old strawberry blonde with freckles just starting her freshman year at Brown University. The groom was a twenty-five-year-old elementary school teacher attracted to the younger, personable teenager, with an infectious laugh and ready smile.

In sixty-one days, I cycled over four hundred miles, spent twenty-six hours on trains, and about four hours on boats, touring seven Western European countries and fifty-four cities and towns. Countless conversations with friends and acquaintances were intellectually stimulating and fun. It was like a college semester abroad, without the credits. I learned about art, foreign cultures, architecture, and geography, and, more importantly, life. I grew from an immature frat boy into a man with global sensibilities. Snapped spokes and a bent tire rim foreshadowed a broken spirit and an altered course that awaited me four years later.

Personal relationships were maintained, rekindled, and awakened. My feelings about love, commitment, and trust surfaced as I observed two kindred spirits get engaged. Physically, I was in the best shape of my life. My tanned body was toned and fit from the daily walking, hiking, and cycling. An unshaven face morphed into a full beard that framed handsome and confident features. I was ready to conquer the world!

Chapter Two

"North to Alaska"

The 1979 Memorial Day–weekend weather forecast called for wind and rain, but that did not deter three cheechako fishermen determined to catch the first king salmon of their lives. Pat, an Irishman and coworker, his Pennsylvania father-in-law Sonny, and I, loaded our gear into a de Havilland Beaver turboprop. The float plane was known as an Alaskan pickup, because of the state's lack of roads. We flew into the Alaskan Bush with a cooler of beer, a gun, a camera, tents, sleeping bags, food, fishing gear, and an inflatable raft. We planned to land on a south central Alaskan lake and float down a river for three days until we reached the river's mouth. There, we hoped to reunite with our pilot, bearing a cooler full of salmon, stories, and photographs.

Fishing was as lousy as the weather for the first two days. Our first day was especially challenging when our raft hung up on a sweeper log that knocked Pat, his camera, and gun into the frigid river. With his Irish temper flaring, he climbed back into the raft, cursing his bowmen for not warning him as he fished in the stern with his back to the sweeper. Sonny and I sheepishly apologized and quickly set up camp and started a fire to dry his clothes.

Despite wet wood, we coaxed a fire from a match, toilet paper, and kindling. With larger pieces of wood, it burned hot enough to dry clothes and warm our shivering bodies. Beer and food lifted our spirits as we pitched our tents and climbed into our sleeping bags for the night. We awoke to a smoking fire and more rain as we prepared the morning

15

coffee. After breakfast, we broke camp, loaded our raft, and prayed for improved boating, weather, and fishing.

The second day, Sonny got the first bite of the trip. Although jealous of his luck, Pat and I were glad for the older outsider, who traveled across country for the adventure. While Sonny battled his salmon, Pat and I quickly reeled in our lines and helped Sonny land his fish. I helped steer our raft out of trouble while Pat reached for the net. Unfortunately, Sonny had lightweight fishing line more suitable for small trout than Alaska king salmon. As a result, the bright silver king broke his line as Pat attempted to net it. Now it was Sonny's turn to vent his anger on his son-in-law for not netting the fish quicker.

The sun shone brightly in a sky full of puffy white clouds as we floated to the river's mouth. We beached our raft, donned waders, and fished from the bank as we waited for our ride back to Anchorage. Pat hooked the next fish and landed a shiny male chinook salmon so fresh it had Cook Inlet sea lice on it. Soon after, I landed a larger female king (would that make it a queen salmon?)—not as fresh looking as Pat's, but a greenish silver-and-red trophy nonetheless. I was ecstatic since it was the first king salmon and the biggest fish I caught.

Tired from lack of sleep and muddy from our wilderness adventure, we flew back to Anchorage with a cooler full of salmon and empty beer cans. I arrived home to an empty house and immediately put my gutted, slimy, and somewhat stiff fish (from rigor mortis) into a bathtub full of ice. When I showed my catch to Carol, she congratulated me but immediately ordered the fish removed from the bathtub, cut, and packaged for the freezer.

The best catch Carol and I made in Alaska lived in amniotic fluid for nine months, rather than Alaska's famed fishing habitat. Rachel, conceived in the Yukon Territory, was born in May 1980, after a bumpy drive in Hatcher Pass induced labor. Christopher, our son, was born Thanksgiving weekend 1981, a planned cesarean, which was the last predictable thing that has happened in his life.

We did not let young children interfere with our annual fishing rituals. To accommodate a growing family, we bought a Jayco pop-up tent camper in early 1980. On summer weekends, we packed the trailer with food, fuel, and diapers and towed it with our four-wheel drive Subaru station wagon. We drove down Seward Highway to fish Seward for silver (coho) salmon, Russian River for red salmon (sockeye salmon), and Whiskey Gulch for king salmon (chinook salmon). Memorial Day halibut fishing in Homer became an annual family adventure.

Our favorite destination for catching red salmon was the Russian River, near the town of Kenai and Soldotna. When Rachel was an infant, Carol carried her in an all-in-one vinyl padded crib, changing table, and diaper bag, complete with mosquito netting to keep away the bugs. We hiked along both banks of the Russian to find holes where the fish rested on their long journey upstream to spawn.

Using flies and a weighted line, I kept my hook floating downstream, hoping to snag a fish in the mouth. The fish did not bite, because they had gorged themselves in saltwater and, once in freshwater, were only interested in reaching their spawning grounds. Some days, it was easy to catch the limit of three fish, ranging in size from six to eight pounds.

After landing them onshore, I unhooked them, held them by the gills, and killed them quickly with blunt force trauma or a stab wound to the head. To keep them fresh and edible, I removed their heart, lungs, and intestines and kept them on a stringer, cooling in the river. When we got back to our campsite, I iced them in a cooler and processed them at home with an electric carving knife.

The first halibut and the heaviest fish I caught was in Alaska, during Memorial Day weekend 1981. My US General Accounting Office (GAO) Anchorage Office coworkers and I chartered a fishing boat out of Homer, and each of us caught two halibut, the state limit. Each of the fish caught weighed between thirty-five and over one hundred pounds.

In calm waters, between Halibut Cove and the Homer Spit, I muscled in a forty-pounder on an eighty-pound test line. I fished the bottom with herring, a heavy lead cannonball weight, and a large barbed hook that would make Captain Hook proud. For fifteen minutes, I slowly pumped the heavy-duty pole up and down against the boat's railing while reeling in the fish close to the boat's stern. One of the deck hands gaffed the whitebellied, charcoal-gray body while two closely spaced, bulging eyes stared at me.

When Pat hooked the one-hundred-pounder, it took about thirty minutes to reel it in, where it could be gaffed and placed on the deck. The boat's captain pointed the nozzle of his shotgun close to the fish's head and pulled the trigger to prevent the fish from thrashing around and breaking someone's leg.

In August 1981, my mother, wanting to see her first granddaughter, convinced my father to fly her and three of my brothers to Anchorage. My youngest brothers, Charlie and Wayne, were thirteen and about to enter high school. Paul was fourteen and dating his first serious girlfriend. My father was fifty-six and my mother, fifty-four, with five children still in the nest.

Prior to their arrival, none of my immediate family had been to Alaska. With my two years of Alaskan residency, I provided guide services to popular fishing spots, north and south of Anchorage. We all took the car train from Portage to Whittier, where we boarded the Alaska ferry to Valdez, via the Columbia Glacier.

All avid fishermen, my father, three brothers, and I drove north toward Palmer and the Matanuska Valley, to the Little Susitna River. Fortune smiled upon us as Mount McKinley made a rare appearance behind a parting curtain of pinkish clouds. Coming from flat New Jersey, my guests could not believe how massive the mountain appeared. We left the main highway, and I put my Subaru into four-wheel drive to navigate the hilly, rutted, and dusty Burma Road.

Mount McKinley Majesty

The five Bresky men spread out along the river after hiking through tall boggy grass. Charlie got the one and only bite of the day. He yelled, "Net!" after a ten-pound silver took his hook. Since Wayne had the one and only net, he waded upstream against a strong current and stumbled toward Charlie. Meanwhile, Charlie played the bright fish close to shore but lost him before Wayne could net the fish. Despite feeling disappointed and annoyed with his twin brother, Charlie was still glad to have hooked his first salmon.

The next Alaska Bresky fishing adventure had a better outcome. The five of us drove to Seward and fished for pink salmon from the bank. My dad and each of my brothers caught salmon that day. I was excited to share a successful Alaskan fishing experience with them.

In 1982, we traded in the Jayco pop-up trailer for a larger Coleman tent trailer in time for a winter visit from Carol's parents, who lived in North Carolina. Worried about my elderly and infirm father-in-law traveling through snowbound Turnagain Pass, Carol's father surprised us with how delighted he was when we stopped there for a picnic lunch next to six-foot-high snowdrifts. Wilbur Larson wanted to visit his old Baptist missionary friend, who he worked with in Alaska. His friend lived in a small rustic house on the Kenai Peninsula, heated by chunks of coal scavenged from a conveniently located coal seam. My in-laws slept in their friend's house while Carol and I tried to keep a two-year-old and a four-month-old warm in a tent trailer with a malfunctioning propane heater. Zipping four sleeping bags together, we relied on body heat and extra blankets to avoid frostbite. Christopher cried most of the night, despite drinking warm breast milk. We all thawed out in the morning

To ensure equal access to Alaska's marine bounty, Carol and I took turns fishing while sharing child care. One Homer excursion in summer 1982, I provided Daddy daycare while Carol fished for halibut. To entertain Rachel and Christopher, we went to a city park and playground. I pushed them on the swings, alternating between each child like an athlete competing in synchronized pushing. When the swings lost their appeal, Rachel and Christopher took turns sliding down a tall metal slide. I sat at a picnic table supervising their play. Christopher liked to test his older sister's patience by refusing to dismount the slide quickly. Screaming at her brother to move, Rachel lost her balance and fell backward to the ground. I rushed to her aid after witnessing this recreational rage.

Rachel cried while trying to catch her breath. While I comforted her, Christopher ran over and feigned an apology. Thus was the start of his successful acting career. Rachel, in no mood to forgive, scolded Christopher loudly until her tears subsided. Rachel suffered emotional but no physical damage. However, she made sure Carol heard the whole story, when she returned from fishing, and how the whole incident was Christopher's fault.

Visits from East Coast relatives continued in May of 1983, when my brother Douglas joined us from New Jersey. While Carol, the kids, and I slept in our camper, Douglas slept outside in a small tent very close to the busy and narrow one-lane Homer Spit road. Noisy pickups and motor homes disgorged campers and fishermen at all hours of the night and kept my brother's sleep to a minimum.

Douglas's luck worsened the next day, as our charter halibut fishing boat encountered rough seas. He spent most of his time on the water puking (chumming) over the side of the boat while I caught both of our quotas. Before he went home, we made sure he carried plenty of frozen fish to share with family in Jersey.

In August 1983, I participated in Seward's Silver Salmon Fishing Derby. I was the only fisherman on an all-day charter boat that caught a coho. It weighed over ten pounds, too small to win any prize money.

Not all of our trips to Seward resulted in fishing success. In September 1983, the family and I towed our fourteen-foot Avon inflatable raft and outboard motor to fish in Resurrection Bay. Two adults and two small children squeezed into our boat as we launched from the Seward dock. I steered while Carol and the kids trolled for salmon.

Weather conditions worsened as steel-gray clouds rolled in on moderate winds. Sea chop splashed water into the raft, and saltwater spray soaked our faces. Without a single bite, I decided to steer us back to shore. That was when our Johnson outboard motor suddenly stopped. I pulled the engine's starting cord and adjusted the choke without any luck. After ten futile minutes, Carol exercised her arm muscles until she gave up. Despite our life jackets, we started to worry.

Wet and cold, Carol and I took turns rowing us towards the shore. With a strong headwind and stronger outgoing tide, we made little forward progress. Luckily, several boats in the area noticed our plight and motored over to assist. We told the fishermen about our failed motor, and they offered to tow us to shore. Relieved to be rescued, we thanked our fellow boaters as we reached dry land. On the car ride home, Rachel and Christopher excitedly talked about our adventure while Carol and I thanked God we had survived.

Our family's most successful fishing trip in Alaska occurred on Memorial Day weekend 1984, when Carol, Rachel, Christopher, and I camped with another neighborhood family at Whiskey Gulch. Located on the Kenai Peninsula between the towns of Kenai and Homer, Whiskey Gulch was a rocky beach camping area along Cook Inlet. From the highway, it was only accessible by four-wheel drive vehicles, because of its rutted, steep, and sandy entrance road. We shared our neighbor's large motorized inflatable raft and trolled north and south along the Cook Inlet shoreline. Dressed in yellow rain slickers, green waders, and black rubber boots, we fished herring with a flasher in shallow water. Carol caught the heaviest king salmon, weighing about sixty pounds, while I caught three bright silver chinook, weighing between ten and thirty pounds. I gave the biggest one to Rachel as a birthday present.

Rachel's Birthday Present

Have you ever been to a place where grizzly bears outnumber humans? The summer of 1984, my brother Douglas and I visited such a place called McNeil River State Game Sanctuary and Refuge in southwestern Alaska. McNeil River originated from glaciers and alpine lakes in the Aleutian Range. As the river flowed toward the lower Cook Inlet, it provided sustenance to an array of wildlife, most visibly salmon and brown bears. The Alaska State Legislature designated the McNeil River area as a wildlife sanctuary in 1967 (and enlarged it in 1993) to protect the world's largest concentration of wild brown bears. One hundred forty-four individual bears frequented McNeil River each summer to feed on salmon.

The sanctuary protected about two hundred square miles of wildlife habitat and was located approximately two hundred air miles (four hundred kilometers) southwest of Anchorage and one hundred air miles (160 kilometers) west of Homer. It was a wilderness area with no roads or development. The Alaska Department of Fish and Game managed the wilderness area to protect the brown bear population and limited daily visitors to no more than ten, from June 7 to August 25.

After a delayed takeoff from Anchorage due to high wind and weight concerns, our float plane flew over St. Augustine Volcano while we watched a golden sunset reflected off a mirrorlike Cook Inlet. At dusk, we landed on McNeil River like a water skier completing a jump. Our guide and assistant greeted us and introduced us to the six other permit winners.

Armed with a shotgun, bear whistle, and spray, our guides led us on daily one-and-a-half-mile hikes through sedge grass, gravel, and gray sticky mud to McNeil River Falls. Although the falls have attracted up to seventy-two bears simultaneously, the most I counted was twenty.

A sow (female bear) watched her two yearlings play in the tall green grasses. Another mama grizzly taught her young cub how to swim and catch fish. Adolescent bears fought each other while defending fishing holes. The older and heavier males, big enough to withstand the powerful waterfall, impaled flying chum with serrated teeth and dissected them with their sharp claws. Other bears herded fish in shallow water with padded paws that looked as large as hockey goalie mitts. Once the bear corralled a salmon, he peeled off its skin with his teeth and surgically removed its eggs. With plentiful fish, the gourmet bears dined on caviar appetizers and left salmon sushi for less discerning bears and seagulls. Like a snorkeler, one bear poked its nose in a shallow pool and surfaced with a fish firmly clamped in its jaws. First standing and then sitting, it devoured the entire salmon, balanced between its paws.

Sarah Palin and Bristol

No bears attacked or threatened us during our three-day trip. The bears mostly ignored us since we stayed on well-established trails and did not threaten them or their food. Our guide never used his gun to scare or injure a bear. Rather, when one bear got too close, he raised his arms over his head and yelled to keep the bear at a safe distance. To prevent a bear mauling, the guides advised against approaching a sow with cubs or fishing within sight or smell of feeding bears. At the camping and cooking cabin, we securely stored food while we ate and slept. To avoid attracting bears with tempting aromas, we could not cook certain foods, like bacon.

A professional wildlife photographer, Leonard Lee Rue III, joined us on our trip. He packed lots of camera gear and film and shared some of his pictures and knowledge with us. I was impressed with him and bought his book entitled, *How I Photograph Wildlife and Nature.*

To pass time between visits to the falls, we played cards, fished, and sweated in the sauna. The bears caught more chum salmon than I did. I was not too disappointed, because chum or pink salmon are not as prized as silver, red, or king. Alaska Native Americans only feed chum salmon to their dogs, so chum are also called dog salmon. Southeast Alaska fishermen are marketing them to consumers under the name *keta* salmon. They are easy to catch, but their bony and soft flesh do not appeal to me. I guess I am a salmon snob.

Douglas and I slept in tents, close to the cooking cabin, so we could quickly run to a secure location if and when bears entered camp. Although none walked through camp, it was difficult to sleep, because the loud bear grunts sounded closer than they were. For two nights, I was so nervous that I sat in the cooking cabin reading and writing rather than sleeping.

As our float plane took off and ferried us home, I reflected on the sights and sounds of my visit. Anxious to develop my fifteen rolls of film, a mental slideshow flickered before my closed eyes. Large and small, male and female bears with names like Waldo (eight hundred pounds) and Snaggletooth (oldest) flashed to mind. Sounds of glaucous gulls and rushing water accompanied images of swaying green grass and black rocks covered in bird poop.

In January 1985, Carol, Rachel, Christopher, and I took one of our last Alaska trips before moving to Oregon. We flew to Juneau, Alaska's capital city, in the southeast part of the state. From Juneau, we boarded an Alaska ferry and sailed to Haines to witness the largest gathering of bald eagles in the United States.

Every winter, hundreds of bald eagles flock to the Chilkat Bald Eagle Preserve to eat salmon from a river kept ice free by underground thermal springs. In twenty-degrees-below-zero weather, the eagles targeted their prey from leafless trees or by circling above a frozen white landscape bisected by a ribbon of steaming water. Like an airplane practicing touch-and-go landings, the birds swooped down with daggerlike talons and smoothly speared a wriggling salmon before taking off to land on the riverbank.

The powerful talons severed the salmon's spinal cord, after which the eagle's yellow beak tore the fish into edible portions. With bears in hibernation, the eagles had the salmon all to themselves, with the exception of gulls, tourists, and other raptors.

Photographing this winter spectacle was challenging. To avoid damage to my camera and film from subzero temperatures, I stayed in my heated rental car and shot many pictures through an open window. When I had to exit the car to get a better shot, I left the engine running so Carol and the kids remained warm and I could thaw out my body and equipment when I returned. I also replaced film rolls in the warm car, nestled in my down parka, to avoid turning my film brittle, like a breakable icicle.

The sun shone brightly in a deep-blue sky, and winds remained calm during our three-day stay. We slept in a comfortable Haines hotel, with hearty breakfasts and dinners. Everybody enjoyed the adventure, and I photographed stately bald eagles in their natural habitat at close range. It sure was a lot more fun than going to the zoo.

Out On A Limb

Alaska changed me from a downhill to a cross-country skier. When "lower forty-eight" downhill ski friends heard of my defection, they sarcastically suggested I choose a small country. There are many Nordic skiers in Norway, Sweden, and Alaska. Anchorage high schools had Nordic ski teams that competed on groomed and lighted trails all over the city. Cross-country skiing kept me in shape throughout long Anchorage winters, and friends convinced me to join the Alaska Nordic Ski Club and compete in recreational races.

Born in Anchorage, Rachel and Christopher enjoyed the sport, even before they could walk. I pulled them behind me in a sled with a black fiberglass bottom and an orange cloth-covered top. They sat bundled up behind a plastic windshield, sitting in a wood-backed seat. Once they learned to walk, Christopher, Rachel, and I cross-country skied on public trails that connected our housing development to east and west Anchorage.

Sometimes, I skied with my border collie named Zero, who helped pull me along icy trails, his leash attached to my waist. Much like dog sledding, it is called skijoring. Other times, I skied by myself at night on lighted high school trails. One night in southeast Anchorage, I survived an encounter with a large female moose and her two calves.

Due to my Alaskan experience, rainy Northwest winters, and my Norwegian heritage, I continued to cross-country ski after moving to Oregon in 1985. During winter weekends and school breaks, Carol, Rachel, Christopher, and I drove to Mount Hood National Forest to enjoy its many nice cross-country ski trails. My favorite was Teacup Lake, because of its varied terrain, dry snow, and good mix of intermediate and expert trails. The Oregon Nordic Ski Club grooms several Mount Hood cross-country ski trails and accepts donations for the cost.

It was a hazy, crazy, and lazy day after Thanksgiving. With a brain as foggy as the weather, I absentmindedly served breakfast to my large-nosed Labrador, Zeus, in a narrow tin coffee can scoop, rather than in his easily accessible wide-mouthed plastic bowl. I did not realize my error until Zeus greeted me at the garage door wearing a coffee can muzzle. I laughed while apologizing.

My twenty-seven-year-old son, Christopher, and I planned to exercise off our holiday gluttony by cross-country skiing at Teacup Lake. I returned home from an early morning oil change to find him fast asleep. I woke him up with loud music and flashing lights. Motivated more by my excellent ski and weather report, he opened his eyes and headed to the shower. After I fixed us a hearty breakfast of egg burritos, we drove east toward Mount Hood, which beckoned like a snow-covered paradise.

Cascade Mountain Magic

The drive lasted over two hours. Because of hazardous driving conditions, we stopped to put on tire chains. Lying on a cold, snow-packed turnout, fumbling with tangled metal chains while tractor trailers and speeding SUVs splash snow and ice on your prone body was not my idea of fun. That's why I brought my son along. I drove, and he agreed to put on chains.

Local FM radio stations entertained us on Highway 224 as we cruised out of Carver through Barton and Eagle Creek before we stopped in Sandy for rental skis, boots, and poles. Rock 'n' roll compact discs kept us alert, when radio stations faded out. We passed a traffic *jam* in Welches, blinding *lights* in Brightwood, and a juke *joint* in ZigZag.

Surprisingly, the Teacup ski area parking lot was empty. Once on the trail, we only heard squawking ravens and gliding skis as we breathed heavily uphill. Dressed in layers, we removed one layer at a time as our bodies overheated. Being early in the ski season, only a foot of snow covered the trail. Later in the season, six-foot snowdrifts buried the outhouses.

Waxless rental skis, suitable for above freezing conditions, swished on crystallized snow glistening from the bright sun. At temperatures lower than freezing, Nordic skis required wax for optimum glide. We herringboned upward and gradually ascended the hilly terrain, stopping for air and water. Like teens on a roller coaster, we yelled and hollered down the hill called Screamer.

At the bottom of Screamer, we skied an unmarked side trail but quickly turned around when it circled back toward our starting point. I felt tired, like an athlete who "hits the wall" during a long race. I concluded that my fatigue was caused by the higher altitude and lack of conditioning. My gracefully lithe and physically fit son, on the other hand, urged me on, toward expert trails in the woods. Instead, I insisted we stay on the safer and flatter main trail.

Parts of the main trail passed through a crystal cathedral of snow-clad evergreens. Every so often, we heard and saw clumps of snow warmed by the sun rain down, leaving bare green branches and white confetti-filled air. The magical show reminded me of shaking a snow globe and waiting for the white flakes to settle.

We stopped for lunch and spread our food and water bottles on the blanket of snow. Sitting on a sturdy and bare tree branch, we hungrily ate our tasty combination of leftover salmon (also the name of a local rock and roll band), rice, and teriyaki vegetables. Gray jays begged for handouts and signaled the end of our lunch break.

Christopher led and I followed in his tracks. Imitating nature, he playfully dislodged an avalanche of heavy wet snow from a low-hanging branch. Enjoying the snow shower, he suggested I photograph him posing under a larger snow-laden branch. I borrowed his camera and clicked several photos of him covered in white frosting. Later, he took a photo of me skiing next to snow-painted evergreens that towered along both sides of the trail. His picture captured how humbled I felt skiing among God's creatures, white and tall.

Mount Hood National Forest

Later, while we stopped for a water break, Christopher shouted loudly to see if his voice would echo throughout the surrounding valley. To both our delights, his voice echoed three or four times before it was swallowed by the white countryside. It sounded like a worried mother calling for a lost child.

Our slippery sojourn continued across a hillside until the trail turned steeply upward, toward the main trail. Before the steep ascent, we faced the bright sun to tan our faces and warm our bodies. With our arms propped up by poles stuck in the snow, we looked like cormorants drying their wings.

To prevent slipping backward, we climbed the hill with our skis in a V-shaped pattern. The ascent was slow and gradual, and when we reached the highest point on the main trail, I thought of my mom. In sight of Mount Hood, I said a silent prayer in her memory. She learned to cross-country ski at Mount Hood Meadows during a family visit to Oregon.

My mother must have heard my prayer, because she watched over us on our return drive down the mountain. Rounding the corner of a sharp icy curve, my lightweight Toyota Corolla spun around in a circle and plowed, hood first, into a snowbank. Thank God, neither of us were injured, and the car was not damaged.

Nervously, I drove to Sandy to return our rental skis at Otto's Cross Country Ski Shop. The owner, noticing laminated price tags on the bottom of my skis, asked me if they interfered with my sliding and gliding. I said I did not notice the tags or felt any difference skiing on them. She told us about a customer who used duct tape to slow down his girlfriend's skis on a steep downhill trail from Mount Hood's Timberline Lodge. I joked, "My chained tires could have used some duct tape on the icy drive down the mountain." Christopher laughed.

Just like two months in Europe changed me from a boy to a man, my seven years in Alaska turned a man into a father. I learned more about love from my wife and children during family outings. Alaska's beautiful land and bountiful fish and wildlife deepened my connection to nature and respect for the environment. Visits from family and sharing travel memories awakened brotherly and parental love. Experience with a subsistence culture dependent on hunting and fishing opened my eyes to the Native American experience and made me more appreciative of those who live off the land and grid, leaving a smaller environmental footprint.

Chapter Three

"Oh, Canada!"

To escape the July 2002 days heated by climate change and to try a new vacation experience, Carol and I booked a Carnival cruise to eastern Canada. After first visiting my parents in Scotch Plains, New Jersey, we boarded an 11:45 a.m. New Jersey Transit railcar in Fanwood. In contrast to the old, dusty, and hot trains I rode into Manhattan as a youth, our train was modern, clean, and air-conditioned. We changed trains in Newark and arrived at New York's Penn Station, dragging large suitcases.

We hailed a cab outside Penn Station and asked the driver to take us to the Passenger Cruise Terminal. He demanded to know the exact pier number as we motored toward our destination. I looked through my travel documents but could not find a pier number. Since we had time until our ship sailed, I suggested the cabbie drive to the southern end of the terminal and head north to look for our ship.

Grudgingly, he followed my suggestion but launched into a diatribe against Carnival Cruise Lines for not giving us specific pier information. His loud voice and caustic tone was so irritating, I wished we had hailed the *Cash Cab*. This guy was wound up tighter than my sphincter muscles during a prostate exam. Cool as a cucumber, Carol did a cell phone shout out to Carnival, who answered her question with a multiple-choice answer. Because the company operator did not know the location of a ship the size of a small city, she gave Carol three possibilities.

Arriving at pier ninety-two, I told the cabbie to stop when I spotted our ship named *Victory*. Glad to escape from the Grand Inquisitor, we wheeled our luggage through a sea of people crowding the terminal. Noisy traffic, rude joggers, and lines everywhere blocked our path. With backpacks and suitcases, we rode the wave of tourists inside the terminal.

A Carnival representative carrying a clipboard stopped us. She said we could not pass through US Customs until we checked our luggage with the porters. Like rafters caught in an eddy, we were sucked into a whirlpool of passengers circling around beleaguered porters.

One porter, pushing a mountain of bags on wheels, offered to take our baggage when he returned with an empty cart. Expecting him to find us among the huddled and befuddled masses, we awaited his return. Recognizing us, he loaded our suitcases and led us to the Carnival registration and US Customs lines.

After sweating in line, we handed a young man our booking information and passports. He greeted us and retrieved our computerized reservation. Curious about the size and capacity of our ship, I learned it was about one thousand feet long and carried twenty-five hundred passengers. After checking in and clearing Customs, we received our Fun Sail Credit Cards, room keys, and identification tags.

Since we could not enter our cabin until our luggage was delivered to our room, we spent an hour touring the ship and eating lunch. The food on the Lido Deck, next to the pool, reminded me of a Las Vegas buffet. I sampled a little bit of everything, including roast beef, salads, fruit, soft ice cream, and iced tea.

Our room number, 1014, meant it was on the tenth deck, fourteenth room, on the left side of the boat. Picking up our luggage at our cabin door, we entered our spacious stateroom with a king-sized bed, private balcony, and plenty of storage. I saw the bridge from our balcony and could hear the ship's foghorn loud and clear. The stateroom had a bathroom with shower, a small couch, a table, cabinets with drawers, and a television. What luxury compared to the ocean-crossing accommodations afforded immigrants and slaves!

At 5:00 p.m. on Saturday, July 20, the Carnival *Victory* debarked. The sun broke through the afternoon haze, and the Big Apple's skyline and Statue of Liberty gave us chills as we sailed under the George Washington Bridge. Prior to this voyage, the largest vessel I had been on was a ferry. Like everything else in New York City, the Carnival *Victory* was larger than life.

While Carol and I toasted each other with champagne on our balcony, our next-door neighbor, Vinnie, introduced himself. Hearing the volume and pitch of Carol's voice as she excitedly named the passing sights, Vinnie joked that she keep it down during our midnight sexcapades. Fortunately for Vinnie, but unfortunately for me, Carol's seasickness curtailed carnal cavorting.

The Pacific Dining Room was abuzz with activity and conversation as we found our assigned dining table for the early dinner seating at 5:45 p.m. The eight-person round table had a great view of the ship's bow. We introduced ourselves to tablemates Jim and Jan, originally from New Jersey but now living in more affordable Pennsylvania. Jim, with his Sergeant Bilko crew cut, and Jan, with her stylish short blonde hair, were delightful dinner companions. They said they were on their second cruise, so we asked them for advice.

The couple seated to my left was also from New Jersey. Phil was a retired accountant, and Anne was a registered nurse. Phil resembled the actor Richard Dreyfus, and he mentioned he had heard that from others. The last couple to be seated at our table was Bob and his girlfriend. Bob was a former marine, and he proudly wore a marine medallion around his neck. He drank like a fish and loved to sing. His girlfriend enjoyed gambling and was an artist. They lived on Staten Island, home of the bars I frequented in high school.

Our waiter, Vladimir, was from the Czech Republic. Most of the crew, including the captain and his staff, were from countries outside the United States: Bali, Philippines, Germany, St. Vincent, and Italy. One of the classical musicians who entertained passengers in the Neptune Lounge was French. I felt like I was on a floating Epcot Center. The food was gourmet quality and reflected the international flavor of the crew. Our appetizers, entrees, salads, and desserts were much better than the descriptions in the Frommer's and Lonely Planet's reviews. After dinner, Carol and I watched a Broadway musical revue performed in the opulent Caribbean Lounge. The venue had a large stage with a full-pit orchestra. Inlaid marble dolphins danced next to an octopus-tentacled chandelier hung from the ceiling. We sat in the balcony in comfortable theater-style seats. Carol thought the sound was too loud while I enjoyed both the music and dancing.

Our cabin's location was convenient for pool and entertainment activities but more subject to the pitching and yawing of the ship. Twice, as we sailed through rough North Atlantic and Bay of Fundy waters, Carol and I were jarred awake by turbulent seas that nearly tossed us out of bed. Three out of the five days, we sailed at between fifteen and twenty knots per hour with seas considered slight (one to two-foot waves or swells) and calm winds. The other two days and nights, seas were moderate (three to seven-foot swells) with higher winds. Days in port were mostly sunny and mild while weather at sea was often cloudy with hazy sunshine. The fog crept in on cat's feet during the evening and stayed until morning.

Day two, still full from the previous night's scrumptious dinner, we decided to order a light room-service breakfast. Later, the cruise director gave a humorous PowerPoint presentation on our touring options while docked in St. John, New Brunswick, and Halifax, Nova Scotia. His delivery reminded me of Will Smith.

After a buffet lunch, I went to the outdoor pool to try out the waterslide and watch the Hairy Chest Competition. Not a big fan of body hair, Carol rested in the cabin. While in line at the waterslide, some youngsters assured me that the slide was not fast and that the water was not cold. They were correct about the slide, but the sixty-four-degree saltwater shocked my warm body and convinced me that one ride was enough.

The Hairy Chest Competition was a shock of a different kind. Nine men volunteered as contestants to be judged by three female volunteers. During the first round, each man paraded in front of the judges, allowing them to feel their chest hair for texture, density, and depth. It reminded me of shopping for carpet. The next round, each contestant serenaded the judges with various karaoke tunes. After five contestants were eliminated, the final four danced with naked torsos. The audience voted for a winner with their applause and cheers. Bigfoot won a white Carnival bathrobe. I was glad I did not enter the contest, because for the next four days, Carnival played and replayed the event on the ubiquitous public and private television screens scattered throughout the ship.

Having eaten a light breakfast, I returned to the cabin hungry, so Carol and I had lunch. With the promise of free champagne, I lured Carol to the art auction. We left the auction quickly for the scavenger hunt after learning that the free champagne ran out. We teamed up with a younger couple with Southern US accents and found eighteen of the thirty-one requested items. The winner found thirty items in ten minutes. Not having played scavenger hunt since our children were young, I attributed losing to a lack of practice.

Our second night's dinner featured Caribbean lobster. Our maitre d' sang a Frank Sinatra tune. Meanwhile, our waiter humored us into second portions of appetizers, entrees, and desserts. Not feeling up to a late night, Carol turned in early while I headed for the evening magic show. The magician was funny, and one or two of his tricks impressed me.

While we snoozed, the ship cruised past Maine, through the bumpy and foggy Bay of Fundy to St. John. Pronounced swaying replaced the previous night's gentle rocking, and the persistent foghorn disturbed my restful slumber.

We docked at St. John around 7:00 a.m., and Carol and I had room service again. Disembarking after breakfast, we received a warm and friendly welcome from some of St. John's senior citizens. Female passengers received roses, and male passengers received lapel pins. We picked up a free map and walked along the paved waterfront trail toward Reversing Falls, so named because the St. John's river reverses direction during the world's highest tide changes in the Bay of Fundy. I visualized being on a down escalator that started going up.

The one-and-a-half-mile trail to the falls was mostly level and meandered along the banks of St. John harbor. Walking along the red-bricked pathway, we passed interpretive signs written in French and English. The signs explained the importance of the St. John port to the New Brunswick economy. Besides seeing tourist boats, we saw a red-and-white Canadian Defense Department boat and container ships. Lobster traps and fishing boats also floated in the harbor.

The developed portion of the trail ended about a third of a mile from the falls. It connected to a concrete sidewalk in front of the Canadian Defense Department headquarters building. I kept a lookout for a Canadian Mountie on a water ski.

We followed the sidewalk along a busy highway. Our first glimpse of the falls between the St. John River and the Bay of Fundy was disappointing. As we crossed the highway bridge over St. John River, the view improved with some mild-looking rapids appearing near both riverbanks. However, we did not see anything that resembled a dramatic waterfall flowing backward. Anybody who has lived in the Pacific Northwest for twenty-seven years knows what a waterfall looks like.

When we reached the other side of the bridge, we descended stairs to an observation deck, where we could get a better look. Although the bay's tide was rising, it still was not high enough to reverse the river current. So we decided to have lunch at a restaurant overlooking the "falls" while waiting for the world's highest tide change to overtake the St. John River current.

After ordering our lobster roll lunches and a Moosehead beer, the scenery out our restaurant window got interesting. About two hours before high tide, we saw white water rapids flowing upstream on both sides of the river. While we ate, two tour boats sailed upriver through the rapids. Passengers waved and smiled, and I regretted not booking us on the riverboat tour.

On the hike back to the Carnival *Victory*, I stopped to take several pictures of the reversing rapids. Mist and clouds shrouded the bridge and rapids as dozens of seagulls and black cormorants fished. The sun came out, and rainbow-colored wildflowers enhanced the scenery. We savored the magical moment as we sauntered back to our floating fortress.

Seagulls and Boys

37

Before dinner, we sunned ourselves on our cabin's balcony, above the shimmering water of St. John's harbor. Neptune's voice, sounding like our cruise director, boomed over the ship's intercom. He said that our departure to Halifax was delayed due to a technical issue. *Could their radar be on the fritz,* I thought. *I'll just have to slather on some more sunscreen and bake in this wonderful sun a few hours longer,* I mused.

Fifteen minutes later, we heard bagpipers playing and the ship's engines and propellers starting. Chills ran down our spines as we watched and listened to the kilt-clad buskers sending us off in royal style. We quickly dressed for dinner and proceeded to the Pacific Dining Room.

Waiting to be served, we chatted with our traveling companions. One couple toured the city on a double-decker bus and enjoyed their day. After eating our appetizers and main course, Vladimir served us Baked Alaska. Our maitre d' sang, the waiters danced (some on tables), and we joined in an impromptu conga line around the dining room.

In her scopolamine haze, my wife succumbed to another early night. I headed out solo for the evening show, a musical revue of the '60s, '70s, '80s, and '90s. The show's highlight was its medley of Beatles tunes, sung by oversized foam-costumed dancers resembling John, Paul, George, and Ringo. They also had foam musical instruments, which they enthusiastically pretended to play. I imagined a review of the musical might be titled, "Foam Fab Four Frolicked Frantically."

Because of the technical issue, we arrived in Halifax, Nova Scotia, an hour late. Not wanting to be outdone by their Halifax rivals, the local populace greeted us with a bagpiper, drummer, and marching conductor. The harbor and city dwarfed St. John in size, and local artisans were everywhere.

Carol bought a set of pewter earrings and a moose-antler wine stopper for our Oregon neighbors. For a moment, I thought I was in Alaska, where moose-dropping jewelry and swizzle sticks were popular tourist items. Unfortunately, that was as close to any four-legged Canadian wildlife we got during our trip.

Since the bus tour of Bay of Fundy National Park sold out, we toured Halifax's major tourist attractions on foot. We walked along a waterfront trail before stopping at the Halifax Maritime Museum. We saw an interesting pirate exhibit, complete with a hanging skeleton. However, we spent most of our time touring the *Titanic* and Halifax Explosion exhibits.

Since Halifax was the closest port to where the *Titanic* sank, hundreds of recovered bodies were buried there in one of three city cemeteries: one Catholic, one Jewish, and one called Fairview. At Fairview, grave markers were arranged in a ship's outline.

Between ten-and twenty-five thousand shipwrecks line Nova Scotia's coastline. I sarcastically asked my wife if she would have booked our cruise, knowing that statistic. Reading off of a display, she said most shipwrecks occurred before 1950 and that major advances in shipbuilding, navigation, and radar technology reduced the risks of sailing in Nova Scotia waters. She's a smart lady, with all the answers.

The December 1917 Halifax Great Explosion occurred during World War I, when a Norwegian munitions ship and a British relief vessel collided in a channel connected to Halifax Harbor. Over two thousand people died at sea and on land from the shock wave, ensuing fires, and a tidal wave, which destroyed northern Halifax. The museum's exhibit displayed photographs and videos of the devastation and carnage caused by one of the worst naval accidents in world history. Pictures of the damage reminded me of photos of Hiroshima and Nagasaki. The detonation was so large that US atomic scientists researched the explosion during World War II, when trying to estimate the potential strength of an atomic bomb blast.

Intrigued by the Great Explosion exhibit, I read Hugh MacLennan's novel called *Barometer Rising*. The novel is set in Halifax during the maritime accident and provided details on many of the sites we visited. One of those sites, The Citadel, located on one of the highest points overlooking Halifax, was a strategic fort used by both the French and British. The Canadian government now owns and operates the fort as a tourist attraction, complete with a daily changing of the guard ceremony. The fort also shoots off its cannons everyday at noon.

Before taking the stairs back to town, we posed for photographs with the Citadel guard and walked around the fort, stopping to admire the gorgeous view of McNabb Island and Lighthouse. Colorful trees, bushes, flowers, and manicured lawns, separated by stone walkways, greeted us in a city park. A majestic white gazebo marked the park's center while off to one side was a pedestrian bridge.

We exited the public park and gardens to find the jazz festival advertised in one of our tourist brochures. Not jazzed by the music, we left to explore some of the public buildings and stores along the bustling downtown streets. The architecture of the churches and public buildings reflected the city's British heritage, complete with picturesque gargoyles.

On our last day at sea, we passed by Nantucket Island on our way to New York City. The weather was hazy and foggy, with the sun trying to poke its face from behind a gray curtain. As the foghorn blew, I was reminded of the *Andrea Doria,* an Italian cruise liner that sank near our course after colliding with the Swedish ship, *Stockholm.* What is it with the Norwegians and Swedes? Why did their ships get involved with these accidents? I am sure Garrison Keillor would have an answer for that question.

The year was 1952, forty years after the *Titanic* sank and one year after I was born. For years after the *Andrea Doria* disappeared, ships traveling the North Atlantic Outer Banks threw wreaths in the water to honor the forty-five to fifty who died. Unlike the *Titanic* disaster that took almost two thousand lives, the *Andrea Doria* tragedy had between nineteen hundred and two thousand survivors.

Although I enjoyed most of my first cruising experience, I doubt I would vacation again on such a large boat. With twenty-five hundred passengers, it was difficult to avoid crowds. Also, events, like the art auction, ran out of free alcohol due to the large turnout. Unloading at our two ports of call, I felt like part of an invading army. The food and entertainment onboard were great, but Carol's seasickness ruined part of the experience.

Chapter Four

"No Woman, No Cry"

The Caribbean called, and we answered in 2005. Frequent-flier miles allowed us to book free round-trip flights to the US Virgin Islands for our thirtieth wedding anniversary. Like a golf mulligan, our trip was a do over to make up for a less-than-stellar honeymoon in Florida, when we married in 1975. "Bargain Bob" was my father's nickname, so I learned from a master. However, once on the plane, I realized the economic truism, "There ain't no thing as a free lunch."

I smiled at the flight attendants as I boarded our flight immediately after first class and golden card members. My smile turned to a frown as I settled into my middle seat, next to a passenger with overflowing girth. His overlapping stomach folds qualified as carry-on baggage, better stowed somewhere other than on my left armrest.

This brown mound of many pounds made Charles Barkley look anorexic. He resembled a sumo wrestler or a smiling Buddha. He wore a green felt Tyrolean hat with German/Austrian hiking pins. I could not visualize this guy hiking anywhere without being pushed on a hand truck. He breathed heavily as his friend across the aisle called him Chunky and adjusted the gauge on his oxygen tank.

Squeezed into my bulkhead seat, I felt claustrophobic, despite the extra legroom. The feeling intensified as I frantically searched for my seat belt. Sweat dripped down my nose when I found it in the dark crevasse of Chunky Mountain. I buckled up quickly, wishing I could trade my extra legroom for a wider seat.

Chunky politely asked me if I was all right, and gasping for air, I said, "Yea, at least I'm glad I've got legroom!" Still sweating from the extra body heat, I turned on the overhead air nozzle to cool down.

My uncomfortable situation worsened as passenger 6F wedged himself into the window seat on my right. Not quite as hefty as Chunky, he stowed his carry-on luggage at his feet rather than in the overhead storage compartment. My legroom disappeared as I struggled to keep my right foot off of his briefcase.

Sensing my distress, two angels came to my rescue. A flight attendant told 6F to stow his briefcase in the overhead compartment. Chunky's companion convinced the same flight attendant to move Chunky to another empty aisle seat before his oxygen ran out. Grateful for his friend's suggestion, I moved to Chunky's vacated seat, which was as warm as sourdough in a miner's armpit.

Arriving in St. Thomas, I bought myself a T-shirt for Father's Day. The shirt was an artistic tribute to Bob Marley, king of reggae music. A Jamaican taxi driver offered us a ride back to our condo. "No thanks, mon," I said. "We have a rental car." He turned away in disgust, throwing his empty Red Stripe beer bottle on the grass.

Next morning, we attended a beautiful and moving mass at Charlotte Amaile's St. Peter and Paul Roman Catholic Church. In observance of Father's Day, the priest invited all fathers to the altar to be blessed with holy water. In addition, all fathers received a prayer book and red carnation. The congregation clapped enthusiastically as fathers exchanged handshakes and sarcastic condolences.

I wore the red carnation with pride the rest of the day. My floral badge elicited hearty salutations from many vendors. I felt like I was family.

On Sundays, no cruise ships landed at St. Thomas, so we found few shops open. Carol bought a beautiful blue wrap from one of the street vendors while I got a good deal on a Seiko watch. Carol also bought a sterling silver chain for one of her handmade fused glass pendants.

To the sounds of laughter from the shore, I capsized my kayak about fifteen minutes out on Pineapple Bay. The rental guy and my wife chuckled as I struggled to overturn my yellow life raft. I had the last laugh though, as I spotted a huge yellow-and-brown-shelled leatherback turtle. I hurried ashore to share my adventure after two men on a parasailing boat warned me that turtles bite. After kayaking, we snorkeled off of Cokki Beach. In two hours, we saw yellow-and-blue wrasse, parrot fish, barracuda, trumpet fish, grouper, bar jacks, and yellow tangs. I took pictures of brain coral, fans, and algae shaped like tree branches. Fatigue ended our fun that day.

We traded paddles for sails the next day. The *Fantasy* was a catamaran (two-hulled boat) with a twenty-five-hundred-pound metal keel. Over breakfast introductions, we departed Red Hook Harbor for St. John's Caneel Bay. The four adult passengers sat up on the port and starboard sides while two teenagers shared the cabin with Captain Pam. First Mate Charlie served us Bloody Marys and beer and handled sail rigging.

Pillsbury Sound Sailing

The trip through Pillsbury Sound was exciting. To maintain balance while turning into the wind, passengers gathered on one hull suspended in midair above four-foot swells. Not wanting to capsize, we hung on for our dear lives as waves splashed in our faces. Once we entered Caneel Bay, the wind abated, and the water surface calmed. The captain anchored the boat while I pulled in my trolling fishing line.

Unfortunately the hook was empty, but I hoped to catch a fish on our return sail.

Two hours sailed by as we snorkeled around the shallow coral reefs bordering the Rockefeller's former winter home, now Caneel Resort. The bright blue, green, yellow, and red parrot fish picked algae off the coral, often ingesting both food and coral. Digested coral excreted by parrot fish produce a ton of sand per acre per year.

After snorkeling, we climbed into a small inflatable raft called a dingy so we could move to shallower water. Eyes magnified by glass masks, open mouths gasping, and rubber fins flapping, we tumbled into the dingy like netted groupers. Pam took us closer to the beach, where the currents slowly drifted us back to the anchored *Fantasy*. The four adults swam with two hawksbill sea turtles while the teenagers floated along with two southern stingrays.

Rum punch in one hand and a tuna fishing pole in the other, I prayed for better luck on the sail back to St. Thomas. Napping in the warm sun, I was awakened by Pam's voice yelling, "Fish on!" I reeled in my line, attached to a small silver-and-green tuna. My spirits soared disproportionately to the size of my catch.

Next day, we traded in a sailboat for a car ferry to reach the smaller and less developed St. John, US Virgin Islands. After an hour wait, we jockeyed for position with four other lines of traffic to board the ferry. Without anyone directing traffic, it was a chaotic boarding process. The ferry crossing took about twenty-five minutes, in fifteen-to twenty-five-knot breezes and three-to five-foot swells. During the ride, we sat on benches, trying not to worry about getting seasick from the bouncy waves.

Despite our apprehension about the rough seas, we docked successfully at Cruz Bay and parked our car in a shopping center close to the National Park Service's (NPS) Virgin Island Visitor Center. After lunch, we signed up for the ranger-led hike to Reef Bay and collected some hiking trail information. Then we went shopping for a T-shirt for Carol. The mall we chose was beautiful, with graceful archways, spiral staircases, decorative fountains, and tree-and flower-lined walkways.

In comparison to the mall's architecture, our hotel looked like a hovel. Our St. John Inn room was small, smelly, dirty, and dimly lit. Its view of tidal mud flats contrasted unfavorably with the blue Water Bay view we enjoyed in St. Thomas. A night table missing a leg was propped up in one corner, and the room door lacked a dead bolt. Barking dogs provided security for our trucking company neighbor. Another neighbor sold Jamaican and US beer from his garage while his patrons relieved themselves while walking in the alley behind our hotel.

Our first night in Cruz Bay, we explored some indoor shopping centers while walking to dinner. A dinner of half-priced drinks and fresh grouper preceded more shopping at Powell Park outdoor stalls. Carol purchased an embroidered travel bag while I unsuccessfully searched for a disposable underwater camera. To avoid the hot and humid night, we escaped to our air-conditioned room.

A complimentary Continental breakfast greeted us the next morning while we watched the *Today Show* on a sixty-inch big-screen television. Tom Cruise's diatribe against antidepressants seemed especially overblown on such a large viewing platform. High on life, we packed the rental car with bagels, oranges, muffins, diving masks, snorkels, and water bottles for the drive to Trunk Bay.

Passing Caneel Bay and then Hawk's Nest Bay on Route 20, we stopped at an overlook. Trunk Bay, one of the Travel Channel's top ten scenic bays in the world, filled the windshield and camera lens. Dark-green trees and white-sand beaches framed clear turquoise waters. We stopped for photographs and then continued our journey.

Finding a shady parking space next to the pristine beach, we rented snorkeling fins and beach chairs before heading to the water. Like penguins, we waddled backward into the warm water. Stone trail markers identified the coral and fish swimming along the NPS's underwater snorkeling trail. I photographed parrot fish, tangs, angelfish, trumpet fish, grouper, snook, and grunts.

We returned to our beach chairs for lunch after working up a big appetite. Refueled, we snorkeled again, this time spotting stingrays and sea turtles. One ray, in deeper water, lay motionless on the sandy bottom, with only air bubbles and eyes visible. Nearer to shore, a cleaner fish hitched a ride on a ray's back. Before we quit snorkeling, we saw a small bluish transparent jellyfish.

For dinner, we ate at the Fish Trap restaurant in Cruz Bay, entertained by eight hummingbirds with black bodies and green breasts. The following evening, we drove Route 10 east to Coral Bay for dinner. The trip took longer than planned due to traffic and the narrow, winding, and hilly roads. Almost a dozen wild goats greeted us as we arrived at Miss Lucy's.

Seated next to a couple from Red Bank, New Jersey, we enjoyed a great meal of roasted pork, mashed sweet potatoes with raisins, zucchini, and rice. For dessert, Carol ate key lime pie while I had bourbon pecan pie. We washed the food down with a tropical drink called the Painkiller. To work off the calories, we danced to a blues band.

It was pitch black when we left Miss Lucy's restaurant in Coral Bay, St. John, US Virgin Islands (USVI). Driving a rental car along a narrow, dark and winding road to our hotel in Cruz Bay was scary. The only light came from the headlights of speeding taxi drivers as they passed us in the opposite direction. Out of the tarry colored night, my headlights illuminated a sign for Robertsville. I quickly slowed down as a reflexive response to many years driving on 25 mph roadways through small American towns. Luckily I did because three donkeys slowly crossed the road in front of our car. Carol's face turned ghost white, as I slammed on the brakes to avoid hitting them. A tropical thunderstorm filled the sky with lightning and sheets of rain as we pulled into our hotel parking lot.

Donkey Detour.

Squealing tires, growling engines, and honking taxis woke us the next morning. Breakfast service was late, as our waitress seemed more interested in chatting on her cell phone than setting up our food. As she swept up broken glass pieces, the hotel manager admonished her for leaving the air conditioning running in vacated rooms.

Motoring toward Leinster Bay, we saw seventeenth and eighteenth-century sugarcane plantation ruins. Within an hour, we arrived at the Watermelon Bay hiking trail. Windy and overcast weather, combined with white caps and strong currents, did not bode well for snorkeling. Despite the conditions, we tried snorkeling after a mile walk along the rocky shoreline. Sediment churned by waves made visibility poor. I only saw a boxfish.

Once the sun broke through the dense cloud cover, we warmed ourselves on the beach. Brown pelicans and seagulls plunged into the water for food. Suddenly, Carol yelled, "Turtles!" and I returned to the rough water. Nervous about the strong currents, Carol remained onshore to watch me through binoculars. Less than fifty yards out, I spotted a stingray, gliding along the sandy sea bottom. About one hundred yards out, I eyed a huge sea turtle with a green shell and a brown-and-yellow head and flippers. Virgin Islands National Park is home for two endangered sea turtles, the hawksbill and the green. Female hawksbill turtles come ashore on remote St. John beaches to dig nests and lay eggs. After burying eggs in the warm sand, the female returns to offshore waters. The hatchlings, which instinctively survive human and animal predation, return to the water.

With a deep breath of salty sea air, I descended twenty-five feet to the sea bottom and saw a hawksbill turtle swimming with two remora cleaning fish. One green-and-white remora lay on its back upon the turtle's top shell while the other swam underneath the turtle. My lungs bursting for air, I returned to the surface for some deep breaths. The current carried me from the bay to Atlantic Ocean waters, and I felt tired from fighting its strong forces. To gather strength, I floated on my back for a few minutes before swimming backstroke toward the shore. The turtle followed me to shallower water and surfaced for air, just like a winded snorkeler. It grazed on algae and seaweed before I lost sight of it and three stingrays.

Over lunch, I excitedly shared my experience with Carol. We walked back to the car after red and black ants invaded our picnic. Drenched from a sudden cloudburst, the return hike seemed longer. Our Miss Lucy's dining companions met us along the trail, and we previewed what lie ahead.

Loving history, I drove to Annaberg Plantation to see preserved ruins of a Danish sugarcane mill (slave farm). From the top of a hill, the brick ruins overlooked a mangrove forest picnic site and the distant outline of the British Virgin Islands. The postcard beauty of the mill's sleeping quarters, windmill, horse barn, boiling rooms, and rum distillery masked a profitable enterprise made possible by the blood and sweat of African slaves. Like a spoiled child, I whined when the snack shop didn't serve rum with its pizza.

The crash of thunder, the flash of lightning, and the splash of rain filled the night skies as we tried to sleep. Humbled by the day's sights, I was grateful for having a roof over my head and a comfortable bed. Heavy rain continued until dawn, after which we ate and took a taxi to the Reef Bay Trailhead for a guided 2 2/10-mile hike. The trail began about five miles east of Cruz Bay, on Centerline Road. It descended through shady, moist, and dry forests with varied plant life. The trail passed through remains of four sugar estates and abandoned farming communities.

Before Danish settlers and African slaves worked on St. John sugarcane plantations, the Carib Indians inhabited St. John. In AD 1425, the Caribs sailed canoes, holding as many as eighty passengers from South America, through the Lesser Antilles to reach St. John. The Caribs that Columbus encountered in the Lesser Antilles were skilled seafarers and warriors. They pursued and enslaved resident Taino Indians in extending their territory. While the Caribs hunted and gathered food from the sea, the Tainos made pottery and farmed the land. The Caribs made boats from hollowed-out kapok tree trunks, drank black and wattle tea, and ate sweet nuts and powder from seed pods. Centipede excretions provided a dental numbing agent called phenol. For our snack, we ate mangos and limes from trees that lined the trail. We passed on the phenol until our next dental appointments.

Fearful of the menacing brown termite nests along the trail, we learned of the termite's ecological role in preventing forest fires. They eat rotten wood. A pond carved in a stone grotto served as our lunch spot. As I ate, I meditated over reflected images of ferns and sacred ancestral petroglyphs. In contrast to Hispanic patriarchal societies, the Caribs were a matriarchal society. As great warriors, the Caribs had a reputation for eating their conquests. Although little evidence documents any cannibalism, Hollywood perpetuated the myth in *Pirates of the Caribbean: Dead Man's Chest.*

Petroglyph Pond

Our hike ended at the ocean beach, where we swam to an anchored coast guard trawler, which returned us to Cruz Bay harbor. Duffy's Love Shack served us dinner.

A two-hour power outage spooked us during our last night in St. Johns as another violent thunderstorm shook our simple cocoon. Reading by flashlight and candlelight, I fell asleep, haunted by ancestral spirits perhaps awakened by our visit to sacred hunting or burial grounds.

Ever since our frugal honeymoon in May 1975 when I booked a government reduced rate at a Florida Travelodge, Carol and I decided our 30th wedding anniversary would be more edifying than visiting St. Augustine's Ripley's Believe It Or Not Museum to see the limousine in which JFK was assassinated. Still watching our expenses, we used frequent flyer miles to visit St. Thomas and St. John, US Virgin Islands. Like the Hawaiian Islands we visited while living in Alaska, these

Caribbean Islands exceeded our romantic expectations. They relaxed, rejuvenated and renewed our love for each other and for nature.

Honeymoon Beach

Chapter Five

"Rocky Mountain Way"

Escaping Portland, Oregon's 104-degree temperature in July 2007, we headed to cooler mountain climates. After a two-and-a-half-hour flight, we landed at Denver's International Airport amidst snarling crosswinds, which buffeted our United Airways jet. The landing caused my wife to reach for the Xanax. I encountered worse wind shear taking off from Denver's older airport, Stapleton International. The only time I experienced a tornado was in Denver, when I was there for government business. The GAO office staff evacuated into a concrete parking structure. From there, I saw arcing electrical wires and exploding transformers, when a funnel cloud ripped through the area. Maybe Denver deserved the name The Windy City.

We rented a station wagon and drove to our daughter's rental house in air-conditioned comfort, not having to worry about the dust, heat exhaustion, dehydration, or rattlesnake bites encountered by 1800s-era Conestoga wagons. Concrete sound barriers lined the city's freeways, embossed with tree and leaf imprints. I admire cities that support artistic beauty in otherwise sterile urban landscapes.

We spent our first night in the basement of our daughter's rental house. It was located near the University of Denver. After dinner, we walked around the neighborhood and toured the spacious grounds and Stations of the Cross pathway at the Pope John Paul Retreat Center. Unlike the Stations of the Cross at the forested Grotto in Portland, these stations were surrounded by less sustainable bushes and lawns.

After a scrumptious breakfast at LePeep's, we headed for Granite, Colorado, via the Mother Cabrini Shrine. The visit to the shrine gave me goose bumps. Reading about her life and dedication to the needs of the world's orphan children reminded me of Mother Teresa. Her spiritual presence guided us through the shrine and up the hundreds of stairs to the marble Jesus statue.

On our way to Granite (population seventeen), we drove through Leadville and stopped at its mining museum and mining Hall of Fame. We learned what minerals played an important role in Colorado's history. Two molybdenum (moly) mines operated in the Leadville area. One company was reclaiming its inactive open-pit mine and cleaning polluted groundwater. The other mine was still active.

The moly alloy appeared silver-gray in its raw geologic state. Blasted from the ground, trucks transported it to the mill that further refined the ore. Once processed, moly was mixed with steel to strengthen it. Automobile and aircraft parts both contain molybdenum.

We spent the next two nights in Granite, Colorado, in a log cabin located next to Arkansas Valley Adventures rafting headquarters. The cabin had two double beds, a table and benches, a bathroom with shower, a refrigerator, and a microwave. An electric heater warmed us at night, and fans cooled us during the day. Our first night was relatively quiet when compared to our second night, when we told our rowdy Texas neighbors to turn down the volume of their loud country music. The only thing worse than most country music is loud country music, especially in the middle of the night.

To prepare for our first rafting trip down the upper Arkansas River, we donned wet suits, plastic helmets, and life vests. Encased in tight gray neoprene rubber, we felt like walking sausages topped by colorful yellow, blue, or red helmets. Our guides fitted us with bright-orange life vests that felt as tight as a straightjacket. When a rafter was tossed into the river, guides grabbed them by their vests to rescue them.

Our guide, Krista, briefed us on safety after our van trip to the Arkansas River, Granite Gorge, departure point. She explained how to hold the paddle and what commands she used on the river. We learned how to forward and backward paddle and, most importantly, how to stop from hitting a rock. When wrapped around a rock, we learned to move to the "high" side of the raft and redirect it to the current.

She also explained how to float feet first down the river if we fell out of the raft so we could use our legs as shock absorbers against any rocks or other obstacles. Finally, she showed us hand signals to communicate with each other if we left the raft. Hands on head, patting up and down, meant "okay." Crossed arms on chest meant "not okay" and need "immediate help." Guides pointed to safe areas, where overboard rafters should swim to escape danger.

Our raft included six paddlers and our guide, who sat in the rear (stern) and steered while barking commands. She demonstrated her knowledge and skill on the river, deftly maneuvering our raft through four major rapids named Wake Up, Maytag, Car Crash, and Hopscotch. She said all of the Arkansas River rapids we encountered were Class III, which meant that the rapids required intermediate skill to avoid dangerous situations. Class IV and VI rapids are advanced, and Class V is not passable.

A Colorado River guide later told us that in the Grand Canyon, Colorado River rafters used a different scale (1–10) to rate rapids. The Colorado River ratings indicate how hard the oarsmen or paddlers must work to safely navigate the rapids. I interjected that meant Grand Canyon rapids lacked class. Our passengers and guide groaned.

Halfway through our Granite Gorge trip, we carried our rafts from the river and portaged around a breached dam, built to provide water and power to a Colorado mining company. Once back on the river, waves drenched our blue-and-yellow raft as it bobbed in and out of white-water rapids. The Wake Up rapid was the first Class III rapid and was aptly named. Its fifty-five-degree water temperature felt like a slap to the face. After successfully navigating each rapid, we congratulated each other by exchanging fist bumps with the blades of our paddles. Chest bumps wearing life vests appeared too dangerous. The exciting part of the trip lasted an hour and was a good upper-body workout.

The next day, we drove to Carbondale via Glenwood Springs. The drive through Independence Pass was full of beautiful Rocky Mountain scenery. We saw mule deer and a marmot. In the abandoned mining town of Gilman, I photographed wooden trestles and water pipes used to process moly from a nearby mine.

We met our next rafting guide at the Glenwood Springs resort. After buckling on life jackets and listening to another safety briefing, we boarded a school bus to ride to our Colorado River launch spot. We launched our raft at the Shoshone Power Plant. Unlike the cold, clear water of the upper Arkansas River, the Colorado River at Shoshone Rapids was warmer and murkier. The Colorado was also wider than the narrow Arkansas. Our Colorado River raft held ten paddlers rather than the eight paddlers on the Arkansas. In addition, our Colorado guide used oars rather than a paddle to steer. The most exciting Class III rapids occurred during the first forty-five minutes, leaving the remaining two hours and fifteen minutes pretty mellow.

Near the end of the trip, our guide pointed out areas of the surrounding canyon that burned during a 2002 forest fire. A smoldering fire inside an underground coal mine spread throughout the Glenwood Canyon. Hoping the fire would burn itself out, fire crews ignored it until it jumped the Colorado River and burned part of Storm Mountain. Storm Mountain became the site of a fatal forest fire in 1990, which killed nine firefighters from the famous Prineville, Oregon, hotshot fire crew. According to GAO and public television reports, communication between the US Bureau of Land Management (BLM) Grand Junction Weather Office and firefighting crews was inadequate. Also, fire crews lacked firefighting equipment and supplies. A lightning strike ignited the blaze, and strong winds quickly spread the fatal Storm King fire.

Hot water from Glenwood Hot Springs mixed with the colder Colorado River from bankside streams and underwater thermal columns. As a result, bathers soaked in these warm pools and swam in various stages of dress/undress. We stopped at one swimming pool, where our guide plunged into the river after performing a backward somersault off the raft's bow. Less acrobatically, I joined him in the water, forming my own thermal pool, warmed by the contents of my emptying bladder.

We stayed in Carbondale the next three nights in a highly recommended bed-and-breakfast within walking distance of downtown Carbondale. Our first night, we dined on award-winning Thai cuisine, prepared by a chef written up in *Gourmet* magazine. His food lived up to his reputation. The second night, we enjoyed roasted chicken at Carol's cousin Janet and her partner Russell's house. From their backyard, we saw the Maroon Bells and the vivid red-and-green colors of Red Hill.

Janet Nelson is an award-winning artist, who makes and sells wire sculptures of fish and wildlife. She also creates replicas of Native American art with assorted odds and ends. Touring her garage studio and workshop was like walking through a Wild West museum. Her commissioned rainbow-and-brown trout sculpture was suspended in a local hospital's atrium. We went to its dedication ceremony.

It was easy working up an appetite during our visit to Carbondale and Aspen. We hiked four miles through aspen forests, mesmerized by the Maroon Bells wilderness area reflected in Crater Lake.

Nelson Cousins Hike Maroon Bells

In Marble, Colorado, we hiked to the marble quarry in search of wildflowers. I found plenty of white, blue, and orange wildflowers among massive blocks of 99 percent pure marble. Marble was formed there over many years, when layers of granite compressed limestone layers.

Although one thousand miles from the nearest seaport, this mine provided most of the marble for Washington DC's monuments. We saw one huge alabaster block weighing almost forty thousand pounds (that's twenty tons!). The resulting calcium carbonate or marble is so unique that Italian sculptors come to Marble to carve its precious commodity.

After a scrumptious breakfast of eggs, quiche, fruit, and assorted breakfast breads, we drove from Carbondale to Grand Junction by way of Black Canyon of the Gunnison National Park. The park offered us several short hikes to scenic rim overlooks. We walked through sparse pinion pine and Utah juniper trees to view the majestic canyon walls stained with desert varnish. The staining resulted from magnesium that leached out of sandstone rock layers, giving the canyon walls its reddish-black color. One canyon wall resembled a serpentine dragon head, ready to spew fire from its open jaws.

Lonely Tree

From the Black Canyon of the Gunnison National Park, we drove to Grand Junction, where we spent the next two nights. Our hotel room had a great view of the Grand Mesa plateau and was close to the city's airport. We also found a coin-operated laundry, where we cleaned a week's worth of dirty clothes.

While in Grand Junction, we explored nearby Colorado National Monument, which rose two thousand feet above the Grand Valley of the Colorado River. It was formed when the Uncompahgre Plateau rose high above its surrounding terrain millions of years ago, during the geologic upheaval that created the Colorado Rocky Mountains. We drove the monument's rim road and stopped to hike Window Rock, Canyon Rim, and Devil's Kitchen trails. The trails overlooked colorful canyon walls, fascinating rock sculptures, and the distant Colorado River valley floor.

The largest freestanding rock formation was called Independence Monument. It loomed 450 feet above the canyon floor and was formed when weathering and erosion gradually separated the stone monolith from the surrounding canyon walls. Every July Fourth, local climbers ascend its rugged peak and plant an American flag in honor of the United States' independence from Great Britain.

The next day, we drove from Grand Junction to Durango via the scenic Highway 141, which bordered sections of the Uncompahgre National Forest. The drive took us through Colorado's Grand Mesa, where I stopped to fish the San Miguel River. I did not catch anything. However, the verdant streamside vegetation and red sandstone riverbanks compensated for the lack of fish.

We continued our drive through Placerville, Ridgway, Ouray, and Silverton during afternoon thundershowers. From Silverton to Durango, we traveled the scenic and windy alpine roads through Red Mountain Pass. The mountain pass was named for the rainbow-colored minerals exposed by a mountaintop open-pit mine.

We descended from Red Mountain Pass as the rain showers turned to sun. Arriving at our bed-and-breakfast, barking dogs and our endearing German/Austrian host, Walter, greeted us. He apologized for the broken hot tub as he gave us a tour of the house and led us to our room.

The Country Sunshine Bed and Breakfast, located several miles north of downtown Durango, was in the woods about half a mile from the Animas River. Walter was a gourmet cook and his wife, a retired nurse. Their business slogan was "If the food makes you sick, help is close." The hostess's parents were visiting from California, where they retired after living and working in Queens, New York.

Our first night's dinner consisted of freshly made cheesecake and other snacks. Over some local microbrews, we passed the evening on the house's outdoor deck, watching hummingbirds, wrens, and magpies and listening to the East Coast banter of the in-laws. Their back-and-forth wisecracking reminded me of a Stella and Meara comedy routine. The father-in-law sat on the deck, armed with a water-loaded plastic assault weapon; he squirted the magpies to scare them away from the hummingbird feeders.

Next morning, our breakfast fare included potato pancakes and sausage. Our stomachs full, we headed for Mesa Verde National Park, about a forty-five minute-drive from Durango.

The visit to Mesa Verde National Park was one of the highlights of our trip. The park sat on top of farming and grazing land. Buying tickets for ranger led tours was a bit of a hassle, because of the crowds and ticket lines. However, it was the only time during our two-week trip that we felt stressed by the crowds and having to meet scheduled tour departure times.

A female park ranger led us on an hour tour of Cliff House. The adobe stone and juniper wood collection of structures was perched inside a shallow but cavernous opening located in a canyon wall. The Cliff House consisted of several rectangular houses with flat roofs and small windows. Other communal spaces between the individual houses included circular well-like structures called kivas. These shallow areas contained a fire pit with a ventilation shaft and a small hole in the ground called a *sipapu*. The *sipapu* represented a spiritual portal to the ancestral world of the underground spirits. Six supporting stone columns symbolized the four compass headings and up and down. Ancestral Puebloans used a wooden ladder to access the kiva through a hole in its circular roof.

Ancestral Puebloans built community centers like the Cliff House around AD 1000, after farming and grazing nearby lands. Living in more protected stone dwellings provided safer and drier shelter than living in pit houses or tents erected over shallow holes. We saw several examples of pit houses in the park's excellent museum.

Our next park ranger tour guide reminded me of a marine recruiter. He was tall, fit, tan, and rugged looking. Outfitted in a gray uniform and green hat, he exuded a professional demeanor supported by his vast knowledge. He was also a nice guy, who allowed Carol and I to join his tour thirty minutes earlier than our ticketed time.

He led us through the Balcony House, where the Mesa Verde people lived for one hundred years in cliff dwellings similar to the Cliff House. The Balcony House tour was more strenuous than the

Cliff House tour because it required climbing up and down thirty-foot ladders and crawling through a twelve-foot-long, four-foot-wide, and three-foot-high tunnel. In addition, we squeezed, single file, through narrow-slot canyons to return to the parking lot.

After the Mesa Verde people left Balcony House, they traveled south to New Mexico and Arizona. In New Mexico, they lived in larger communities of cliff dwellings preserved at Chaco and Bandelier National Monuments.

Before we left Mesa Verde, we toured the Spruce House, which was accessible without a guide. Getting tired but still wanting to visit the park museum, we walked partway down the paved path to the Spruce House ruins. I felt like I was looking into a stone dollhouse that had been cut in half. All that was missing were the Puebloan artifacts, like baskets, pottery, and tools, which we later saw in the museum.

For dinner, we met our daughter's childhood friend, who lives and works in Durango. We dined at the Palace Restaurant located in the Durango-Silverton train station, home of the historic narrow-gauge steam locomotive and train. The train used to haul coal from nearby mines before being converted to haul tourists between the mining town of Silverton and the transportation hub, Durango.

After a restful sleep, I awoke early to try my luck fishing the Animas River. Nothing was biting, because the river was running high, fast, and murky from the previous night's rainstorm. At least I got some exercise, walking the one-mile round-trip trail. After another filling breakfast, we departed our bed-and-breakfast with a bag of chocolate chip cookies for the road.

The Colorado highway map did not identify the road from Durango to Alamosa as "scenic," but we still enjoyed the views. We stopped at Chimney Rock in the San Juan National Forest and saw two wild turkeys. At Wolf Creek Pass in the Rio Grande National Forest, we saw the area that gets Colorado's most annual snowfall. A photo radar camera flashed as we passed through a twenty-five-mile-per-hour speed zone while going about forty miles per hour. The speed trap seemed designed to catch vehicles driving too fast during hazardous winter driving conditions. Luckily, we didn't receive any ticket.

During a downpour, we arrived before check-in time at our Alamosa bed-and-breakfast. The bed-and-breakfast was in a 1907 home, complete with an art gallery and a living/dining room. Our hostess was kind enough to let us in early after our rainy four-hour drive. Our small room was on the second floor. To access it, we climbed a long, steep, and narrow stairway with a rickety handrail. Dragging two large suitcases weighing about fifty pounds apiece, we trudged up to our room. Opening the wooden bedroom door, an inviting double bed occupied much of the floor space.

After unpacking, we researched dining options and asked the proprietor for suggestions. Waiting for the lightning and thunder to subside, we studied our walking tour map before heading out to find a restaurant. On our way to dinner, we had to wade through ankle-deep water to reach the local brewpub.

The torrential rains and overflowing drainage systems did not stop us or the locals, who flocked to the brewpub for dinner. The place was hopping (no pun intended), and we were lucky to get a table. Having previously tasted two good Colorado microbrews (Fat Tire and Durango), we ordered the San Luis Valley brewery sampler. None of the samples met the high standards of two avowed "beer snobs" from Oregon. However, the portobello mushroom sandwiches were great.

Since we lacked television, Carol and I entertained each other before falling off to sleep. Unfortunately, I did not sleep well, because of the noise from incessant rain hitting the outside of our window air-conditioner. Earplugs did not help, so I wrote in my journal before falling asleep.

The next morning after a hearty breakfast, we drove to the Great Sand Dunes National Park. We got an early start and arrived at the park's visitor center two minutes after it opened. The sagebrush terrain reminded us of the high desert country in eastern Oregon. We toured the visitor center and walked its short nature trail. I photographed yellow-flowering cactus and other wildflowers.

At 10:30 a.m., we met one of the rangers for a guided tour of the park's Meadows Creek section. Because of several years of drought conditions, the creek bed was semimoist sand. The ranger explained how sand, silt, and soil blew from the San Juan Mountains and settled at the base of the Sangre de Cristo (blood of Christ) Mountains, forming the 750-foot high dunes. Also included in the sand were black particles called magnetite. The ranger demonstrated the magnetic properties of the particles by dragging a silver cylindrical magnet through the sand. The magnet attracted hundreds of whiskerlike black hairs that reminded me of the old plastic and cardboard toys I used as a youth to give a bald head and face, a toupee, a mustache, or a beard.

While temperatures remained cool, Carol and I climbed toward the summit of the highest dune. She carried water, and I carried a camera. Since the sand was not hot, we started bare foot.

Despite wearing hats and sunglasses, the harsh sun's glare, reflected off the white sand, was blinding. Having difficulty seeing and following a trail, we trudged forward in a straight line toward the top. Going was slow, as we frequently stopped to drink water, take pictures, and catch our breaths.

Three-quarters of the way, I chose to take switchbacks to the summit. Carol was too impatient for my indirect route, so she continued in a straight and steady ascent. We both reached the zenith of one dune but were disappointed to see that it was not the highest.

Sweating, thirsty, and low on water, we headed downward. By this time, the sand was so hot we wore sandals. Our descent was quicker than our ascent. We reached the parking lot with aching thighs and calves, stretched, and refilled our water containers.

Our air-conditioned car was an oasis of relief as we drove to our next bed-and-breakfast in Pueblo. The Abiendo Bed and Breakfast, located in a stately Victorian mansion, was in a parklike setting. Inside, a beautiful wooden staircase, illuminated by stained-glass windows, led to the second floor. Hardwood floors adorned the downstairs living and dining areas. After unpacking, we browsed some dinner menus while sipping lemonade and relaxing on the home's wraparound wooden porch.

The hostess served us an early breakfast since we had reservations for a morning Royal Gorge raft and rail adventure on the Arkansas River. Our daughter joined us in Canyon City after worrying about recent flash floods in the area. Despite inclement weather and high and fast river conditions, we enjoyed our rafting, catered lunch, and train ride. We returned to Denver to spend the night with our daughter.

Father and Daughter Bonding

Our last road trip, before returning to Oregon, took us to the Rocky Mountain National Park. We drove the Trail Ridge Road, the world's highest paved road in a US national park. over twelve thousand feet. It took us through three different ecosystems: montane, subalpine, and alpine.

We hiked the Tundra Communities Trail through yellow, blue, and pink wildflowers and saw a yellow-bellied marmot scamper over the rocks and plants. At Iceberg Pass, three elk with brown velvet-covered antlers grazed near the road. A park ranger called them the "boys of summer" on their way to meet the "girls" for the fall rut. Later, we saw the "girls of autumn" grazing in the pine forests and meadows of the lower elevation montane ecosystem. I not only saw the elk but also tasted them for lunch as we ordered elk sausage at the Alpine Visitor Center. Before it started raining, we hiked the Irene Lake Trail and spotted two mountain sheep.

Boy of Summer

To celebrate a great trip, Rachel, Phil, Carol, and I attended high tea at the Brown Palace Hotel in Denver. Accompanied by piano and harp music, we feasted on finger sandwiches, scones, and decadent desserts while drinking delicate teas. Exotic waitresses with foreign accents served up the delicious fare on fancy dishes while peasants drooled from the sidelines.

Carried in by the Navajo winds, we departed from an airport that appeared inspired by snowy mountains and Native American tepees. Our visit was like experiencing a cowboy and Indian-inspired *Cirque de Soleil* show, whose performers climbed and rode through dazzling Western sets. Mountains of sand and rock lifted our spirits. Our souls ascended into the sky on kiva ladders. Our hearts, cooled by rain, made fishing and driving challenging; but wildlife and high tea warmed us with family love.

Chapter Six

Mexico

Seasonal affective disorder reached epidemic proportions during Oregon's winter of 2008. The never-ending gray days spread the blues over moss-covered cities, and low-hanging clouds blotted out Mount Hood's spirit-lifting view. In Alaska, we called it cabin fever and flew to Hawaii. In Oregon, my wife and I flew to Mexico's Yucatan Peninsula.

To avoid the annual bacchanalian rite of passage called spring break, Carol and I traveled to Cancun before Oregon, Washington, and California students crowded the beaches and hotels. Like a steady Caribbean gale, we breezed through Mexican Customs with our luggage. A lovely senorita welcomed us to Cancun's International Airport and asked if we were first-time visitors. Very machismo-like, I answered "Si", and she escorted us to an older gentleman, who worked for the Mexican Tourist Bureau.

A man with an official-looking badge asked us a few questions and offered us five free tours if we sat through a sales presentation at a newly remodeled five-star resort. Always looking for a deal, we agreed and gave him a refundable $50 deposit.

We bought our hotel shuttle tickets and waited while the driver discussed fare information with a Hispanic mother and her three kids. "No tenga cuatro bolletos solamente uno," she said in frustration. Not wanting to delay his other fares, the driver sped away, shaking his head in disgust.

My weary and hungry wife yelled "Stop!" as the shuttle driver neared our hotel. Staff outside the Solymar Resort directed us to the condo office. Like walking a dog, Carol yanked on my leash to stop me from staring at the naked female statue as we boarded the elevator.

The elevator was not much bigger than a pneumatic tube capsule. Our expatriate hostess, Carolyn, was surprised at our early arrival, despite having received two e-mails confirming our arrival time. We chatted with an older couple from Connecticut while waiting for our key. Our hostess was bilingual, switching effortlessly between "New Yawk" English and Spanish to "tawk" to visitors and staff.

Like putting a square peg in a round hole, our first room key did not fit. Another key allowed us entry into our intimate efficiency apartment. I felt like a Mayan archaeologist surrounded by walls with half-hidden clay pots. My wife felt like she was home with sand-colored bathroom and shower tiles that matched ours. However, she balked at the small size of the double bed and ordered me to sleep on the futon the first night. Gratefully, two margaritas, grouper tacos, and a walk on the beach changed her mind.

A dizzyingly high atrium lobby, with green rain forest vines, cascaded like a waterfall as we ordered drinks and dinner. Like parched desert nomads who found an oasis, we gulped down our margaritas and wolfed down tasty tacos. Feeling satiated and a bit tipsy, we listened to the lively sounds of a mariachi band performing their greatest hits.

Inspired by a little girl dancing, Carol jumped up from her lounge chair and posed for a picture with the handsomely dressed musicians. I snapped a photo, signed the check, and we took the lobby elevator to the top floor. Gazing down at the brightly lit lobby was like peering down a glass-walled canyon. A fountain of blue-lit water sent mists upward, keeping green leafy vines well watered. I felt like I was in an urban version of a rural Costa Rican cloud forest.

Our smiling waitress approached as we departed the elevator into the lobby. It was then that I realized I absentmindedly signed the restaurant check instead of charging our dinner. She assumed we were hotel guests when she saw the signature but without a room number she returned to find our table empty. "Lo siento mucho," I slurred and paid the bill with a credit card. Carol and I staggered outside to see, feel, and hear the wind-blown Caribbean surf pounding the beach. With no swimsuits and posted red flag warnings on the beach, we stuck our bare feet into the warm salty water, rather than swim.

Our radio alarm harkened us to freedom the next morning: free buffet breakfast, taxi rides, five tours, facials, and massages. The only catch was attending a resort tour and an auto dealer–like sales pitch. The "time scare" presentation did not end soon enough. With five free tours as booty, we rearranged our itinerary to include seven days of touring, including the two tours already purchased online.

Giddy about saving $1,500 in food, transportation, and tours, we spent some pesos at a local flea market. Amidst all of the trash, we found some quality T-shirts, a hat, a leather belt, a wallet, and shot glasses for our daughter's collection. It seemed the merchandise quality was inversely proportional to the volume and aggressiveness of the merchant. Hogfish and grouper fed us for supper, and we purchased snacks and coffee for breakfast.

From Cancun's hustle and bustle, an ecotour van of American tourists, a local driver, and a guide transported us to one of three national parks in the Yucatan Sian Ka'an Biosphere Preserve. The 202-acre wilderness area, located fifteen miles south of Tulum, contained pristine white-sand beaches, limestone caves, lagoons, mangrove wetlands, wildlife, and ruins. The twelve-hour adventure passed quickly due to the variety of activities (kayaking, swimming, hiking, and snorkeling) and the riotous nature of our twelve passengers.

Sharing a van with Minnesota and Wisconsin couples was like listening to Garrison Keillor telling stories from Lake Wobegon. Their small town anecdotes and midwestern sense of humor kept everybody laughing, despite the long bumpy ride. A traveling circus almost hit us on the last few miles of narrow unpaved road, but our talented driver saved us.

A short path from the visitor's center led to a wooden pier with a thatched roof. We followed our guide and driver, who carried paddles, life jackets, and several kayaks down to the lagoon. Carol and I climbed down a wooden ladder, covered in slippery green algae, into our very stable two-person kayak.

Immediately, we paddled to get a closer view of a school of silvery mullet fish. The shimmering fish zigzagged from one side of the lagoon to the other, leaping out of the water and landing with a splash. Their main predator, the barracuda, hunted them like silver submarines.

In the sheltered lagoon, Carol and I kept pace with the group. However, once we paddled into the wind-driven current, we struggled to keep the kayak straight and moving forward. As the kayak turned sharply, my wife blamed me for not paddling. Her loud commands scared some ospreys out of their nests, where they joined a frigate bird and brown pelican in the sky.

The smell of burnt biceps and abdominal muscles wafted through the jungle air after two hours of hard paddling. Exhausted and hungry, we returned to the visitor center for a snack of tangerines, bananas, nuts, cookies, and cold drinks. Refreshed, we hiked through the jungle to the beach, passing huge termite nests. Bird sounds saturated the midlevel rain forest while Caribbean surf splashed in the wind. White-and-yellow palm fronds parted to reveal a white-sand beach. Crabs and pelicans were the only other beachgoers.

Like vanishing Pacific Northwest old growth forests, only 2 percent of Mexico's tropical rain forest remains due to logging, grazing, and farming. Mexico is home to over 1,000 bird species, 439 mammals, 989 amphibians and reptiles, and about 26,000 plants. The southern state of Chiapas alone has 10,000 plant species, more than 600 birds, and 1,200 species of butterflies. Starbucks Coffee buys coffee beans there.

Sian Ka'an's midlevel rain-forest preserve and surrounding jungles had three trees important to the Mexican economy and Mayan people: (1) the sapodilla or chewing gum tree, (2) the Chechen or Black Poison, and (3) the chit palm.

The wood of the sapodilla tree is very durable and weather resistant. Its sticky white resin (chicle) is used to make chewing gum. The Mayans also used it to create mortar. The Chechen tree's bark contains sap that acts like poison ivy. The chit palm tree is endangered because of its heavy use in building Mayan houses. The Mayans use chit palm fronds to thatch the roofs of their *palapas* (huts). According to Mayans, extract from chit palm fruit is used as a diuretic, nutrient, and sedative.

Mexican forest structure and composition varies. The southern rain forest we toured near Tulum had tropical plants like green agave. Mexicans make aloe lotion from the green agave plant. Northwest from the Yucatan lies Jalisco, famous for the blue agave plant used to make some of the world's finest tequila. Mexicans also use the blue agave plant to make paper, tissue fibers, textiles, needles, juice, wine, vinegar, honey, and sugar. Deforestation threatens the Mayans' ability to make penicillin from forest plants and to treat high cholesterol with mushroom fungus.

While the Yucatan heals, it also kills. Mexico and Australia lead the world in cave diving fatalities. The Yucatan Peninsula is one large flat limestone shelf, rising only a dozen meters above sea level. It is punctuated like Swiss cheese with between five to fifty thousand sinkholes called *cenotes*. These bottomless wells formed as erosion caused large sinkholes that drained into subterranean river systems. Rainwater, purified by the limestone filtration system, feeds the hidden rivers.

Mexican Grotto

Feeling fearless for a fleeting moment, I jumped into the Grand Cenote to join the catfish. Compared to the salty and warm Caribbean water, the *cenote* water was fresh, clear, and cold. Our guide estimated it at seventy-five degrees Fahrenheit, with visibility between twenty-five to thirty feet. Limestone stalactites held tightly to the chamber ceiling, like passengers holding straps on crowded mass transit. Stalagmites erupted from the river bottom, like Gothic minarets. I felt like I was floating through Arizona and New Mexico caverns.

Our underwater pilgrimage took us through domed-ceiling chambers that looked like the moon's surface. Where the water level was high, the ceiling was so low that we surfaced with hands and arms outstretched to avoid hitting our heads. Sunlight entered through three grottoes, changing the water color to blue, green, or clear, depending upon the water depth and light. Each grotto was an altar to Mother Nature, adorned with tropical greenery.

Not since I toured the Roman Catacombs, had I felt the sacredness of grottoes as holy places. In *The Innocents Abroad,* Mark Twain wrote,

> When the Virgin fled from Herod's wrath, she hid in a grotto in Bethlehem . . . The slaughter of the innocents in Bethlehem was done in a grotto . . . The Savior was born in a grotto . . . It is exceedingly strange that these tremendous events all happened in grottoes—and exceedingly fortunate likewise, because the strongest houses must crumble to ruin in time, but a grotto in the living rock will last forever . . . it is one that all men ought to thank the Catholics for.

Besides providing the local population with water for the body and soul, the web of *cenotes* provide spectacular opportunities to explore Mexican geology. We visited a small section of the second largest underground river system (seventy miles long) on the Yucatan Peninsula, managed by Hidden Worlds. We snorkeled, zip-lined, and sky-cycled our way through five *cenotes.* Letting go of the zip-line and splashing into the water was especially entertaining, when one of our overweight traveling companions lost his loose-fitting swim suit upon impact.

If It's Tuesday, It Must Be Belgium or, in our case, Coba (pronounced Co-pa') ruins. Our large tourist bus, while comfortable, lacked the intimacy of our previous day's van. To compound the problem, we chose seats next to the one lavatory. Despite our driver's plea for passengers to only use the bus restroom for local phone calls (*numero uno*), one passenger called long distance (*numero dos*) and left a pungent aroma. He must have used a "smell phone" to make the call.

Our tour guide was a half-blood mestizo (Spanish and Mexican) and reminded my wife of Cubans she met while traveling with her American Baptist missionary father. The guide said there were thirty million mestizos in Mexico, out of a total population of 105 million. Twenty-five hundred years ago, Coba had five hundred thousand residents and sixty-five thousand buildings, making it one of the largest settlements of its time.

Because jungle growth hid most of Coba, it was only recently discovered. Many of its ruins were not restored, but its largest and highest one could be climbed. I made it to the top, where I explored its enclosed temple and photographed three fruit bats, with their pink mouths and black pointy ears. They stared down at me like some Mayan gargoyle as I took their picture. Luckily, my camera lens remained guano free.

Chichen Itza' (mouth of the whale of the Itza' people) was one of several Mayan tribes that included the Puucs and Toltecs. The Chichen Itza' site contained more restored and preserved buildings than Coba, because of the extensive work of American and German archaeologists. The Carnegie Institute in Washington DC started to restore and preserve these Wonder of the World ruins in 1921, and archaeologists continue to uncover and excavate new ruins. Time constraints and a lack of a map prevented us from seeing all of the ruins. However, we saw over half, including: (1) the Pyramid of Kukulkan, containing the tomb of the king and queen; (2) the Ossuary Pyramid, housing the high priest's tomb, (3) Temples of the Warriors, Jaguars, and Bearded Man; (4) Platforms of Skulls, Eagles, Jaguars, and Venus; (5) Plaza of a Thousand Columns; (6) steam baths; (7) marketplace; (8) observatory; and (9) nunnery.

Besides being older and better preserved than Coba, Chichen Itza was larger, covering four and a half square miles. Jokingly referred to by some tourists as "Chicken Pizza," it took 1,200 people twenty-three years to build. Without using wheeled transportation, Mayans moved stone blocks from about twenty local quarries to construct it. The Pyramid of Kukulkan had a ninety-six-step stairway, covered by 862 hieroglyphic symbols, honoring over one hundred Mayan gods. Mayans called their rain god Chac and honored him with statues.

Mayan pyramids, astronomy, mathematics, and language development rank with the Egyptians, Romans, and Chinese cultures. The Mayans used their knowledge of the solar and lunar calendar to plan the exact location and design of its Puuc-and Toltec-influenced architecture.

The 384 steps on the outside of the Pyramid of Kukulkan corresponds to the number of days in the Mayan solar calendar. The Mayans also built a smaller pyramid of 260 steps inside the outer pyramid, based on the number of days in its lunar calendar. During the spring equinox, the sun shines on the stone snake heads lining one side of the staircase, giving the impression that the serpent is moving up the pyramid. The vernal equinox sun also highlights the serpent heads on structures surrounding the Kukulkan Pyramid, further documenting the importance that astronomy played in city planning.

If the Mayans had patents, trademarks, and copyright laws, they would receive license fees from computer giants like Microsoft since they created the first binary number system (0,1), the basis of computer languages.

The Mayan alphabet consists of twenty-seven phonetic symbols, forming the basis of 140 dialects. It is an oral language and can only be written using the Latin alphabet (A–Z, CH). Two million Mexicans speak Mayan, but none can write it.

Animal symbols were very important in Aztec and Mayan culture, religion, and architecture. Today, fervent supporters of American amateur and professional athletic teams worship animal mascots as part of America's sports culture. For example, a duck mascot represents the University of Oregon teams while Oregon State University chose a beaver as its mascot.

The snake or serpent head is the most important Mayan god representing fertility. Stone snake heads, many with mouths wide open, form corners of several buildings. One four-and-a-half-ton full-body snake sculpture sits on top of Chichen Itza's largest ball court. The snake's curved body, adorning one ball-court wall, symbolized infinity and the solar system. To shape their heads to resemble a snake's flat head, young Mayans wore tightened tourniquets, holding flat boards to their skulls. Not even the most rabid American sports fan attire goes that far!

The Temple of the Jaguars and the Platforms of the Skulls, Eagles, and Venus represented the warrior class. During athletic contests at the ball court, warriors used blood to paint snake crosses on their chests to pray for abundance. Without using their hands, warriors competed to see who could move an eight-to ten-pound rubber shot put through a twenty-foot-high stone circle. The first warrior who moved the ball through the circle seven times won. World Cup soccer matches and Olympic events seem pretty tame when compared to the action on a Mayan ball court.

Competitions lasted days, and winners celebrated their victory at a religious ceremony called *Pok-Ta-Pok*. It symbolized a Mayan warrior's transition from the physical to the spiritual realm. Some believe that the defeated warriors' lives were sacrificed in pagan rituals and their bodies deposited in the Sacred Cenote. However, few human remains confirm human sacrifice theories.

Only sixty-five thousand of the elite Mayan society lived at Chichen Itza'. The high priest, king, and queen had the greatest social status. As a result, the high priest enjoyed the best seat at ball-court contests and was buried in a separate stone pyramid called the Ossuary. In American society, where money and power are worshipped, corporate high priests enjoy skyboxes at premier sporting events.

Like royalty from Egyptian culture, the Mayans buried their king and queen in the largest pyramid (Pyramid of Kukulkan), with wealthy symbols like jade-jeweled teeth. The sun, snake, and bird gods were some of the most important Mayan gods, and they came to symbolize the king's spiritual power. Our guide compared it to the Holy Trinity in Catholicism: the Father, Son, and Holy Ghost.

Wealthy traders and merchants made up the majority of the site's inhabitants. They conducted commerce in the marketplace represented by the Plaza of a Thousand Columns. Only 584 columns remain today. Respectful travelers cleaned up before entering the city. They washed their feet in wooden water troughs before entering the site's steam baths.

With modern-day fears of exotic flu strains, antibiotic-resistant bacteria, and mutated viruses, maybe we should follow the Mayan public health model. Besides screening foreign and domestic travelers for security reasons, homeland security and public health inspectors could require travelers to wash their hands and feet, take a steam bath, and pass through a decontamination chamber before entering planes, trains, and other public transportation. In the meantime, I will continue to require my house guests to remove their shoes to protect my carpets.

Mayan Children

Global tourism and Mexican commerce have defiled the religious, historical, and cultural aspects of Chichen Itza'. It is far more accurate to call the site "Cha-ching! Cha-ching! Itza," with its estimated seven hundred vendors who shadow tourists along its walking paths. Although a national park and the Seventh Wonder of the World, it has no park rangers and little crowd control. It is not even owned by the Mexican government, as it would be in the US National Park System. As a frequent visitor to US national parks, I think Mexico has lots to learn about the benefits of federally managed cultural and historical sites.

The Spanish family who owns the land where the ruins are located also owns and manages a hotel there called the Mayland Hotel. In total disrespect to the Mayan culture, this family business used ancient Mayan stones from the Pyramid of Kukulkan to build 40 percent of their hotel. Despite Mayan protests about its commercialization, imperialistic capitalism dominated with little Mexican government regulation and oversight.

Greed is not new to the Mexican tourism industry. Spanish explorers looking for gold destroyed one of the four staircases on the Kukulkan Pyramid. The staircase remains damaged, like an ugly scar on Mayan culture.

More recently, American students on spring break defaced Chichen Itza' ruins, causing significant damage to ancient artifacts. As a result, Mexican tourist authorities are focusing their marketing efforts on vacationing families, who share and respect Hispanic cultural values, rather than on boorish and amoral *Jersey Shore* devotees.

Mayan warriors and Toltec artists made peace, not war, and the result was the city of Tulum. Builders of Tulum used stone platforms to level the uneven Yucatan plain, elevated from the sea, sixty-five million years ago. They built a wall around the city for protection. The twenty-one-square-mile lot overlooks the turquoise waters of the Caribbean Sea.

Tulum, like Coba and Chichen Itza', are located along the Tropic of Cancer, connected by ancient dirt roads. City planners used precise surveys based on trigonometric calculations to lay out buildings and roads. The walled city of Tulum contains restored and preserved ruins that have weathered hundreds of years of punishing Caribbean hurricanes. Well-constructed temples for the high priest and other leaders, watchtowers for security and residential homes, and an outdoor plaza marketplace are all visible. Architecture of the central portion of Tulum represents two styles. The Mayan style is evident from high roofs, false wooden arches, and round corners, while the Toltec style consists of flat and heavy roofs with square corners.

Like the opportunistic Mexican cowbird that scavenges everything, we snacked on snake, armadillo, and iguana meat. Since eating Alaskan caribou sausage, bear, whale, and moose meat, I am more adventurous about trying local game. We also felt a kinship with the cowbirds, known locally as banditos, because they steal human food, much like us taking advantage of free tours, food, and beverages.

The next day, this cowbird felt like a brown pelican skimming along lagoon waters, powered by a thirty-horsepower Honda engine. During some of the turns, I banked the boat into the lead boat's wake with a rush of adrenaline and a loud hoot and holler. We motored our sea horse through mangrove swamps before tying up just off of Club Med's resort. Donning our snorkeling gear, we plunged into the aquamarine tropical water, above the world's second largest barrier reef that stretches from Cancun to Belize.

The reef suffered from two hurricanes, and my wife spotted lots of broken pieces of coral and some dead coral formations. Despite the damage, I found a healthy variety of tropical fish, including blue tang, spotted parrot fish, southern stingray, angelfish, and four-eyed butterfly fish. Most of the sea ferns and giant anemones also looked healthy.

Our guide told us that the beaches along Cancun's twenty-six-mile hotel zone lost twenty-six meters of sandy beach due to hurricanes. In addition, we saw some damaged hotels not yet repaired. Newer hotels trucked in more sand to restore some of the lost coastline.

Booze cruises are to the Caribbean vacationer as wine tastings are to the Napa, California, and Oregon Willamette Valley visitor. Both excursions offer a great variety of alcohol. Like brewpubs in Portland, Oregon, each region in Mexico prides itself on its own alcoholic product. Blue agave tequila from Jalisco tastes great, but it is also expensive. Unless specified, most mixed tequila drinks on booze cruises contain the cheaper stuff that causes hangovers. Our guide jokingly said that Mexicans use the worst (cheapest) tequila to clean engine parts. At one Mayan cooperative, I tried *pulque*, which is made from fermented plants. The locals bragged about its healing and aphrodisiac qualities. It tasted like rotting vegetables and did nothing for my libido.

Our booze cruise to the Island of Beautiful Women (*Isla Mujeres*) lasted thirty minutes. After the free beer and tequila, all the island women looked good to me, as did the lunch buffet. After lunch, a gold-toothed guide took us snorkeling to Garrafon National Park. There, we swam through a dazzling array of colorful fish, some in schools of hundred or more. Silvery tuna and barracuda eyed us warily while huge rainbow fish and wrasse circled beneath us. When our guide started feeding the fish, a cyclone of angelfish, tangs, and yellow-and black-striped fish enveloped us, electrified the senses, and took my breath away (literally and figuratively). The waves and currents carried us past underwater landscapes of brain coral, sea fans, green grass, white sand, and purple tubular plants.

As I climbed back on the boat, I realized I forgot to remove my new leather belt and money pouch. The Mexican pesos weathered the washing the best, followed by my US currency. My traveler's checks were soaked and stuck together but still usable after I dried them out. Luckily, the belt and wallet survived the money laundering too.

The Mayan sun god smiled on us Oregon "web feet" and treated us to an unforgettable tropical adventure. We answered the eternal question, "Does Your Chewing Gum Lose Its Flavor?" Yes, only if you put it on a bedpost, rather than a sapodilla tree. Peace was upon us as we toured great civilizations and floated through a "Magical Mystery Tour" more vivid than any acid trip. We imagined what a high-stakes ball game might look like twenty-five hundred years ago and learned how greed and ignorance destroyed ancient relics. We danced to, rather than feared, the "Apocalypso" to come and discovered a new recipe for bouillabaisse: rum, tequila, *pulque*, armadillo, and iguana. The sacred grottoes recharged my spiritual batteries and connected me to holy places not experienced since Italy.

Chapter Seven

The Taming of the Shrew

Like Lucentio coming to Padua to study philosophy and art, I went to Albany, New York, in March 2008 to sample local art, culture, and history. By way of San Francisco and Chicago, I flew on Zeus's breath to see my son in *The Taming of the Shrew*. The other getting-off Broadway show in town garnered more publicity, as the former New York governor starred in the Shaming of the Screw. In contrast to the progress made in cleaning up Hudson River's water pollution, political sleaze flowed like a toxic oil spill.

Before I got to New York's capital region, I journeyed through Chicago O'Hare, where the flight attendant called out gates for connecting flights-Albany, E-3; Philadelphia, B-4; Newark, C-1; South Bend, B-6; and Indianapolis, B-7. A fellow passenger yelled out "Bingo!" and everybody laughed. With a forty-five-minute connection, I briskly walked from gate B-3 to E-3, looking for a shuttle to take me to the E concourse. I never found the shuttle, but my feet and eyes got me there in time for my flight.

Dressed in thermal underwear because I departed Oregon in bone-chilling cold, I arrived in the sweltering Chicago O'Hare Airport, simmering and smelling like boiled fish. Having no underwear beneath my thermal layer, I went commando style in the terminal restroom, hoping to cool off before my connecting flight to Albany. Seated in the last row of the airplane, I felt like I was on the crowded backseat of a city bus. The aircraft's ventilation system did not work, and cabin temperature rose near roasting. As a cost-cutting move, I feared United Airlines would cook us to serve to their first-class passengers.

Back on terra firma, my first meal was "East Coast" pizza, not readily found on the "left coast." I felt like I was in Little Italy, ironic because it was St. Patrick's Day weekend, but also fitting since the setting for my son's first professional acting role was a Shakespeare play set in Italy.

Loyal members of Christopher Bresky's Fan Club, Rachel and I flew cross-country to see him perform as Lucentio, in *The Taming of the Shrew*. Before meeting my brother Wayne and his family for the play's matinee, Rachel and I watched Albany's St. Patrick's Day parade. Perched in an open parking structure above the Capital Repertory Theater, we avoided most of the cigar and cigarette smoke and sloppy drunks.

Forty-five minutes after its scheduled start, four of Albany's mounted police appeared. One horse painted the street with steamy souvenirs while marchers warily walked around them. Surprisingly, no pooper scoopers followed, just bagpipers, marching bands, fire engines, school and civic groups, and other green-clad pageantry. If this were Portland's Rose Festival Parade in Oregon, clowns would have cleaned up the horse droppings before they cooled.

Spectators dressed in leprechaun hats and green T-shirts proudly proclaimed "I'm an Irish Pub Scout." Another celebrant wore a foam hat, shaped like a huge pint of black Guinness stout, complete with a brown foamy head. Lads and lasses wore green beaded necklaces and staggered from side to side.

One portly woman slipped and fell on her face in a drunken stupor. Her less tipsy girlfriend helped her to her feet. Partygoers with green beer in hand walked on horse poop, oblivious to the sticky brown mess covering their shoes. A guy wearing a sombrero did a Mexican hat dance around the equine droppings. I felt like I was in New Orleans for Mardi Gras, without the exposed female breasts. However, one gentleman, when asked to show his nipples, raised his white T-shirt and massaged his man boobs. Female onlookers asked to see more while my daughter yelled for the full monty.

The festivities lasted for well over an hour, after which Rachel and I returned to our hotel to get ready for *The Taming of the Shrew*. We wove our way back to the theater, dodging smokers and drinkers, gawkers and winkers. Retrieving our tickets at the box office, I called my brother, who was driving from Ithaca. Wayne, his girlfriend, Stephanie, and her son, Sam, were late due to traffic. The play started late, so they did not miss anything.

This version of the bard's play was set in the 1950s, with period costumes and Mafia family overtones. The cast was strong, especially the two leads playing Katherina and Petruchio. Well-choreographed fight scenes showcased the cast's physical skills while their verbal parrying elicited much laughter. Lively music and quick costume and set changes moved the action crisply through intermission.

During the break, Rachel and I chatted with Wayne, Stephanie, and Sam. When Stephanie and Sam tried to bring drinks and snacks back to their seats, one gray-haired usher stopped them. Seeing other theatergoers returning to their seats with wine and coffee, Stephanie complained about the seemingly unfair treatment. Fairness and persistence prevailed as patrons passed through portals previously prohibited.

The play's cast paraded across the stage like a more organized and scripted version of Albany's annual tribute-to-Irish pride. Shakespeare's characters, dressed in business suits, black-tie formal wear, and student casual vied for the audience's attention. Three couples found wedded bliss at the play's end, and I stood to applaud the cast's efforts, especially my son's inspired performance. I felt proud of him and happy to see him get paid for work he loved. His sister and other family members were equally enthusiastic.

Since Christopher had an evening performance, he couldn't join us for dinner. Instead, he recommended several restaurants. The first restaurant was crowded with a long waiting list, so we went with plan B. Like hip urban skateboarders, we rolled around North Pearl Street parade trash, beer-guzzling partygoers, and discarded pizza slices.

Our group of five passed Starbucks and turned right up State Street in search of Lark Street. Rachel complained about her aching foot while Stephanie's hunger pains echoed Sam's. We never found Lark Street, so we turned around at one of the city's impressive government buildings and retraced our steps. Cold, hungry, and tired, we entered Crowne Plaza's Kelsey Irish Pub. There were many drinkers, some diners, but very few waiters. I felt like we were late to the party but stayed anyway.

Ten minutes elapsed and nobody came to our table. I volunteered to find some staff but came back with five menus instead. Another ten minutes passed and still no waiter. I retrieved silverware, wrapped in green napkins, and let a waiter know we'd like to order dinner. A half hour after entering the restaurant, Wayne hunted for assistance after I threatened to go to the kitchen and cook our orders. Fifteen minutes later, we placed our order with an exhausted-looking waiter, who was finishing his twelve-hour shift. Too tired to write, he committed our drink and food requests to memory and vanished.

About thirty minutes later, another waiter brought food and drink for everyone but Sam and I. Finally, the last two orders arrived, but only Sam's was correct. Hungrily, I settled for the free grilled Reuben, instead of the gyro sandwich I ordered. Stephanie shrewdly got 25 percent more off our bill, because of the long wait and inaccurate bill.

We left the restaurant, grateful for the socializing, despite the dreadful service. Christopher and his two friends, Stacey and Chris, met Rachel and I for Palm Sunday mass. We walked to the Cathedral of the Immaculate Conception in briskly cold weather. I was impressed by the oldest example of Gothic architecture in the United States. The church's flying buttresses, vaulted archways, and stained-glass windows reminded me of St. Patrick's Cathedral in New York City and the Washington National Cathedral in Washington DC.

Having an itch for a healthy breakfast, we ate at the Scratch Bakery. Besides being Palm Sunday, it was also the National College Athletic Association (NCAA) Men's Basketball Selection Sunday. While Rachel and Stacey discussed natural family planning and fertility charts, Chris and I ate dinner while watching March Madness pairings. Newspapers advertised vasectomy sales in anticipation of the basketball tournament. Their sales pitch went something like "get clipped to lower your seeding."

Sunday's clouds gave way to fading rays of light as the sun set behind the Albany hills. The scenery reminded me of the Hudson Valley School paintings I studied in college art history classes. Monday's bright blue sky and sunshine came at a price of bitter-cold temperatures and windchill. The bank thermometer registered thirty degrees Fahrenheit as we set out for a walk along Albany's art-lined pedestrian bridge and the Hudson Valley walkway.

Rachel, Stacey, Christopher, and I walked about two miles along red brick and black asphalt pavement. I photographed what remained of the Great Basin lock connecting the Erie Canal to the Hudson River. This major river way opened in 1825, providing a transportation and trade route between New York state and Lake Erie. It was immortalized in Pete Seeger's song, "Fifteen Days on the Erie Canal," a song covered by Bruce Springsteen.

On the return walk, we stopped at several exercise stations to do pull-ups and push-ups. The fresh air and exercise stimulated our appetites, which we sated at the delicious Albany Pump Station restaurant.

Shakespeare's themes of love and marriage, appearance and reality, comedy and tragedy proved prophetic. Rachel left Albany to get married in Denver in August 2008. Eliot Spitzer left Albany to atone for infidelity in Manhattan. An Irish pub was not the best place to celebrate St. Patrick's Day. Christ's triumphant appearance on Palm Sunday was overshadowed by the tragedy of his passion and crucifixion. Comedy prevailed through Irish songs and a fun parade and play.

Chapter Eight

California Scheming

During my son's last year (2008) at the University of San Diego's Graduate School of Fine Arts, I returned his car from Oregon by driving it to Southern California. Taking scenic detours to Death Valley National Park, Ventura, Palm Springs, Catalina Island, and the Channel Islands National Park, the road trip inspired both poetry and prose.

Westward bound, they followed the trail,
Upon prairie schooners, they sailed.
Verdant dreams appeared in the night,
Miners went south, farmers bore right.

Straining gravel, looking for flakes,
Following streams into the lakes.
Shovel and pick, tools of the trade,
Mules stumbled on, fortunes were made.

Assayed nuggets sparkled their eyes,
Thousands followed to seize their prize.
Choosing southern brown over northern green,
Mining ore made men lean and mean.

Gold played out, helped by lead,
Fighting broke out, many were dead.

Copper demand rose then decreased,
The mines shut down, the towns deceased.

Urban corpses in watery graves,
Gaze on lake boaters making waves.
Scarred hillsides and abandoned caves,
Flooded for replacement-wage slaves.

Three rivers damned for crops and amps,
Killed sacred fish and Native camps.
Mighty Ag and Bureau of Wreck,
Toasted the projects from their decks.

Brown land turned green with concrete rain,
Canals fed farms and farms raised grain.
Grain made food for man and beast,
Both making waste that never ceased.

Brown behind, planet blue ahead,
Salty sea breeze clears my head.
Seeking redemption from man's sins,
Soon to be cleansed in the ocean.

Sea lions gather on a buoy,
Breakwater rocks white and gooey.
Cormorants dive seeking their prey,
As the captain's boat spews up spray.

California gulls fly wing to wing,
"There's a whale," an Asian girl sings.
Two teens blow chunks over the railing,
Bouncing through swells, we go sailing.

Gliding across Saint Barb Channel,
Temperature's fine if you wore flannel.
Zona campers hug to stay warm,
Boat horn sounds to awake or warn?

Scorpion Landing, our first stop,
Day-trippers, campers unload lots.
Coolers, kayaks, people galore,
Dawdlers are the last out the door.

Next port is Prisoner's Bay,
Our leader Jean shows us the way.
We spot two humpbacks, mom and babe,
Spouting, diving, feeding away.

Guide, teacher, and mother of one,
Jean makes the hike lots of fun.
We see fox scat, eagles, and hawk,
Jean teaches science as we walk.

Lover's Cove is the place to go,
To snorkel with the Calico.
Bread crumbs feed the hungry sea bass,
While laughter comes from lad and lass.

Floating through kelp looking for fish,
I spot rockfish getting my wish.
Orange Garibaldi swim by,
A black-and-green crab says "Ojai!"

Mother, daughter, father, and son,
Come to Catalina for fun.
Lovers embrace in surf and sand,
Swaying to sounds of Nature's band.

Underwater, camera in hand,
I aim at the fish, coral, and sand.
Topsmelt, rock wrasse, halfmoon, and perch,
Opaleye and tide make me lurch.

In answer to the ticket handler's question, "Triple A, AARP, senior discount?" a gray-haired gentleman waiting to board the Catalina ferry said, "At ninety-five years old, I have them all!" I chuckled at his remark as I bought my ferry ticket from Catalina Island back to the California mainland.

The high-speed passenger ferry service was very modern and comfortable, compared to the Virgin Islands ferry system. Inside, cabin seating was better than first-class airline seats, with great views, lots of legroom, a plasma TV, full bar service, and comfortable armrests and cushioned seats. Within an hour, I was back to my hotel at Dana Point.

As I checked in at the front desk, the tall broad shouldered receptionist hit on me. She eyed me up and down and coyly said, "Wow, it sure just got hot in here! Please, won't somebody open up a window?" This woman was too young for menopause and its "summer moments" (hot flashes), so I smiled and took her words as a compliment. She then asked me if her new haircut made her shoulders look too big. Her athletic shoulders reminded me of a swimmer, and I said they looked fine. Heading to my room, I saw an older woman wearing a T-shirt that said I Love Boys, with a swimsuit bottom that featured a smiling yellow face with a protruding red tongue. Now I know the inspiration for the television series *Cougar Town*.

At dinner that evening in the marina, I eavesdropped on a conversation that sounded like a job interview between a thirty-something man and an older woman. He talked about studying music in college and being a drummer in a touring band. He said he injured his wrist just before embarking on a cross-country band tour. Despite getting medical treatment and physical therapy, his wrist did not heal, resulting in chronic pain. Western medicine-trained doctors ruled out chronic fatigue syndrome and fibromyalgia. So he sought alternative treatments like acupuncture and chiropractic medicine. The chiropractor tested his blood for vitamin deficiencies but could not find any that would cause chronic pain. He rehabbed his wrist and met some teenagers, who inspired him to seek a job teaching music. Although I had several things in common with this person (chronic pain and teaching), I was too tired to remain for the rest of the story.

Stark Joshua trees growing in an inhospitable desert-and-sage habitat lined the road to Death Valley National Park. Drawn to a deserted house, with only gnarly trees as neighbors, I stopped to take some digital pictures. As I opened the driver's side door, I found a silver Olympus digital zoom compact camera on the road's shoulder. Coincidentally, it was the exact same model and make as my camera. I checked to see if the camera worked and if its memory card had pictures. To my surprise, the camera worked, but it contained no images. I wondered who owned it and why it was left there. Was this an accident, or was foul play involved? Because the camera lacked any owner identification, I decided to keep it and give it to my wife.

The timing of my discovery was fortuitous because my black camera's rechargeable batteries ran out. Consequently, I used the silver camera to photograph the Trona Pinnacles on federal land near Death Valley. Shaped like cones, ridges, and gravestones, these white rocks formed when volcanic hot water and the mineral trona rocketed through a dried lake bed and cooled.

Feeling hungry, I stopped for lunch in the town of Trona and learned it was a company town founded to mine trona ore, a valuable ingredient of borax and potash. Borax is a white crystalline salt with an alkaline taste used as a flux in soldering metals and to manufacture glass, enamel, artificial gems, and soaps. Potash is used to make fertilizer and soap. Before trains moved the borax to market, mule teams transported the ore. Thus, the product name 20 Mule Team Borax was born. Railroad builders wanted to change the product name to Three Elephant Team Borax once railcars with elephantine power moved the product to market. I'm glad they stayed with the mules, iconic symbols of the Old West.

Tired as a mule from the six-hour drive to Death Valley National Park, I arrived at my hotel, hoping to relax and watch the College World Series Game between Oregon State and California State, Irvine. To my dismay, my room lacked a television and air-conditioning. A noisy swamp cooler and rickety overhead fan were poor cooling substitutes, especially in 115-degree heat.

Hungry as an elephant and thirsty as a desert nomad, I ate pasta and drank a large glass of beer for dinner. Baking from the sun's heat, I crawled back to my room like a lizard. I recharged my camera and internal batteries before touring the park in Christopher's air-conditioned car.

Following National Park Service recommendations, I drove toward Furnace Creek and Artist's Drive hiking trails. In 1849, pioneers on a shortcut to the California gold fields found the springs at Furnace Creek. In the 1870s, the first white settlers, Andrew Laswell and Cal

Mowrey, entered the Furnace Creek valley, looking for water to grow food crops and alfalfa for the booming nearby mining towns. By the early 1880s, Laswell and Mowrey were gone, and the William Tell Coleman and Company owned the Furnace Creek water rights. Coleman built Harmony Borax Works just north of Furnace Creek because his chemical-processing company needed springwater to extract borax from the ancient lake beds.

Through the 1920s and 1930s, the borax companies that controlled Furnace Creek diversified into tourism. US Borax convinced National Park Service officials that Death Valley was a unique national treasure and should be preserved due to its natural and cultural history. In 1933, the federal government created the Death Valley National Monument, which later became Death Valley National Park.

On the road from Panamint Springs to Furnace Creek, I viewed some of the park's natural beauty in the warm glow of fading sunlight. I passed tawny dunes rising to one hundred feet, with late afternoon light accentuating the sands' ripples and patterns. I saw the Salt Creek trail leading to the home of the federally endangered Devil's Hole pupfish, which survived in water as hot as 112 degrees Fahrenheit.

By the time I reached the Furnace Creek Visitor Center, it was closed. Hoping to at least get a colorful and informative park brochure in exchange for my fee, the self-service machine only gave me a white paper receipt with an expiration date. It was 8:00 p.m. and getting dark when I headed back to Panamint Springs, but the temperature was still 107 degrees.

I followed road sign recommendations and turned off my car's air conditioner to prevent engine overheating. For cooling, I opened the car windows and drove fast to maximize air circulation. As I reached 105 miles per hour, I wondered how many other motorists ignored posted speed limits to keep cool without air-conditioning. Furnacelike wind sandblasted my face as I turned up the radio and marveled at the star-filled sky.

Stars twinkled brightly as I returned to my hotel for the night. Getting to sleep was difficult even with earplugs. The swamp cooler's metal fan blades sounded like they scraped the sides of an undersized aluminum barrel every revolution. The resulting horror movie soundtrack mimicked a desert sandstorm. That howling sound combined with the squeaky overhead fan would have pleased slasher-movie fans. It bothered me.

A breakfast of eggs, bacon, and pancakes filled my tank; and I gassed up the car before I departed the Panamint Springs Resort. To describe my lodging as a resort took a real stretch of the imagination, unless you compared it to the primitive campground across the street.

Like an altar boy selected to serve Mass, I answered the call of Father Crowley Vista's scenic viewpoint as its sign beckoned me from the open road. Father John Crowley, a Catholic priest and padre of the desert, ministered to Owens Valley inhabitants of all faiths from 1891 to 1940. He helped defuse tensions and violence that marked the Death Valley water wars.

The landscape of dark lava flows and volcanic cinders abruptly gave way to the gash of Rainbow Canyon. I did not see any rainbows or water, but I did see an F-16 fighter jet zoom by, banking its wing as it entered the canyon. The jet was at my eye level, when it made its *Top Gun* move through the rocky chasm. As I walked back to my car, I talked to a fellow traveler, who had been buzzed from behind by another jet pilot that morning. "It sure got my attention and woke me up," he said with a throaty chuckle.

The flyby incident reminded me of a story I heard during one of the annual Hillsboro Air Shows in Oregon. The Blue Angels were in town, and one spectator said he knew one of the pilots. As a practical joke, he asked his F-16 pilot friend to buzz one of his golfing buddies on a local golf course. As the golfing buddy approached a green for a crucial putt, out of nowhere roared a low flying F-16. I bet they did not have to water or fertilize the greens that day.

Death Valley National Park's 3.4 million acres was impossible to explore in one day. I looked forward to returning there to view spring wildflowers and other sites. However, with nonrefundable hotel reservations in Palm Springs, I left the park and headed in that direction.

I retraced my route through Trona, where I stopped for lunch at the town's outdoor visitor center. Tourist signs explained that trona extracting, processing, and transportation plants provided most area jobs. Replicating nature's thermal geysers, plants injected hot water through pipes into several different soil layers lying 250 feet beneath Searles Lake. The pressurized water flushed out a salt and trona mixture, filtered to separate saltwater and trona solids. Huge white piles of beachlike sand created trona dunes, not to be confused with Lorna Doones. The briny runoff evaporated in bird-protected ponds, periodically dredged of muddy tailing piles.

Rock hounds discovered crystals in these piles worth $100 during gem and mineral society sponsored digs. Hundreds of people annually run amuck there to recover valuable clear-and-pink crystalline rock clusters. To avoid ruining good clothes, the muckers dressed in "sacrifice clothing" that turned to cement when the crystal-laden mud dried. Discovery Channel's *Dirty Jobs* television show documented one such event.

Saying good-bye to starched overalls, I said hello to Palm Springs' wind-driven turbines. I learned that thousands of Coachella Valley homes got their electricity from whirling blades that resembled modern windmills. Don Quixote would have a tough time battling these towering behemoths. Perhaps he would have found strength and sustenance from the avian sushi sliced by massive turbine blades.

Having left what felt like cremation temperatures in Death Valley, Palm Spring's cooler 112 degrees dared me to walk barefoot to the pool. *Ooh! Aah!* Was I wrong. The unshaded cement patio seared my soles as I skipped to the nearest lounge chair. I quickly threw my stuff down on a table with a green umbrella and jumped into the pool. When I got out, I put my feet in a towel sling to shield them from the intense heat. Journaling until sweat beads appeared over my body, I swam one more time before returning to my room.

The hotel desk senorita suggested I eat dinner at the Thursday-night street fair. Walking up and down several blocks of music and jewelry and candle vendors, it was so hot even the store awnings were sweating (actually, they were misting). More in the mood for Mexican rather than a vendor hot dog, I chose an air-conditioned Mexican restaurant with live music. The margarita, fajita salad, and rock-and-roll oldies were a good choice.

Facing another oppressive day of valley floor 112-degree heat, I reasoned it would be much cooler at eight thousand feet above the city. So I headed for the Palm Springs Aerial Tram, also featured on a *Dirty Jobs* television episode. The Swiss-built red-and-blue tram cars made climbing up San Jacinto Mountain easy. The floor of our tram car rotated 360 degrees on the ten-minute climb. There were no bad views in these glass-enclosed cars, and the ride was fairly smooth, except for the occasional bump when passing over a guide tower.

Not being an engineer, the audio-taped guided tour bored me with the mechanical and structural details of building the tram. Of more interest to me was the geology of the rocks and the biological habitat types encountered at different elevations. One rather large rocky outcrop reminded me of the rocks I had seen in Gunnison National Park in Colorado.

Once at the summit, the view of the Coachella Valley was terrific. I gazed out from the observation area at sun-baked Palm Springs, Hot Springs, Rancho Mirage, and other valley communities. Through thermal air currents, I saw shimmering images of the San Bernardino Mountains and Salton Sea. I was glad to enjoy these scenic vistas from an eighty-degree forest, rather than from the 112-degree valley floor.

I toured the San Jacinto State Park Visitor Center exhibits and watched a dated video about the park. After getting a trail guide from the elderly volunteer ranger, I hiked the three-quarter-mile Nature Trail and the one-and-a-half-mile Desert View Trail. Along these trails, I saw the Jeff tree, with bark like a ponderosa pine's and the smell of vanilla. Also, I photographed a sugar pine and meadow oak tree.

The Desert Trail had three overlooks, the last of which was spectacular. On the way back, I spotted three old-growth pine trees and saw blue birds nesting in the cavity of a snag. The Nature Trail contained interpretive signs and meandered through a forest meadow. Wood markers identified the trail names, and colored rocks lined both sides of the trail.

After finishing my hike, I returned to the base of San Jacinto Mountain and drove to San Diego. Hungry and tired, I hit construction traffic in Moreno. Since I was low on gas, I pulled off the highway shortly before the I-215 junction. I filled up with ARCO gas and bought a car wash. What happened next was surreal.

I punched in the car-wash code, but no green light signaled to enter. So I went to the cashier and told her my problem. She gave me another code to try, which still didn't work. The manager came out and told me there was no green light as indicated on the sign but to just "follow the white light." Despite being not ready for a near-death experience, I tried again, and this time a white light flashed. So I entered the car-wash area. Thinking I had to steer my left front tire into the guide rail, I drove the car over the rail, wedging my front tire stuck. Nothing happened, so I started to feel nervous and trapped.

Meanwhile, the driver waiting behind me gave up and left. I sheepishly went back to the manager and told her what happened. She came out again, surveyed the situation, and suggested three options: (1) back up out of the nonfunctioning rail, (2) drive forward, trying to escape the rail using my vehicle's front-wheel drive, or (3) call a tow truck. I chose option two, and it worked. Now the car was where it was supposed to be but still dirty!

Finally, another employee came out from the store with a new wash code. She directed me to drive my front left wheel into a metal box. After I did that, "I saw the light," and the car wash began. After what seemed like an eternity, I left the car wash, ate, and hit the road.

After this midsummer nightmare, I was glad to be seated in San Diego's Old Globe Theater to watch my son play the riotous drunk, Froth, in Shakespeare's *Measure for Measure*. The stress of my journey disappeared as I laughed at his comic antics.

A coyote greeted me the next morning outside my son's apartment, but he refused my invitation for breakfast. Christopher and I ate at the Ocean Beach pier and watched surfers and fishermen enjoying the ocean. I left Christopher's car behind after sharing with him the details of my road trip. As I boarded my flight back to Portland, Oregon, I suggested he hand wash his car the next time it got dirty.

Chapter Nine

"Do You Know the Way to San Jose?"

Tired about reading the morning paper news about how my country's president justified our involvement in another senseless war, my wife and I cashed in some frequent-flier miles and headed for Costa Rica, whose souvenir T-shirts brag about not having an army since 1952. My baggage carried the ashes of my parents, the first people to inspire me to visit Costa Rica, because of its climate, scenery, and people. Despite or because of my father's World War II experience, he appreciated a country that spent more on education, environment, and health than war. He and my mother visited Costa Rica several times, and my dad often talked about retiring there.

Frugal like our Depression-era parents, my wife and I ordered tap water when the drink cart appeared at our aisle. That was the only free drink available. We already paid $15 for each of our checked bags, so we did not feel like getting ripped off further. After all, we flew on the airline that announced shortly after our return home that they would start charging for pillows and blankets.

Not wanting packed leftovers during our layover, we found food in Phoenix before boarding our five-hour flight to San Jose, Costa Rica's capital city. I wondered how many passengers thought they were going to California. After landing in San Jose Airport at 8:00 p.m., we retrieved our luggage and breezed through Immigration and Customs.

Our tour operator drove us from the airport to our hotel. Tired and hungry, we checked in to the Barcelo Palacio Hotel and took the elevator to our room. Not finding any light switches, we stumbled around in the dark, trying to switch on free-standing lamps. No luck! Thinking it was a fuse problem, we contacted the front desk and found the dinner buffet.

Food was plentiful and delicious, some of the best variety on our trip. We introduced ourselves to the tour director, Tony, who told us the time for the next day's breakfast and tour-bus departure. We returned to our brightly lit room, activated by a key card. Illuminated but tired, we fell asleep.

After another filling breakfast buffet, forty-six passengers loaded our Mercedes cruise ship on wheels to tour sights in and around San Jose. Our first stop was the Juan Santamaria drummer boy statue. Made in France to celebrate Costa Rica's national hero, it marked the heroic act of a young soldier during the country's battle for independence from Spain in 1821.

In 1502, Spain discovered and claimed Costa Rica and sent indigenous Incas, Mayas, and other Carribes to Spain as slaves. Costa Rica encouraged European settlers to emigrate, and many Jews sought refuge there. In search of gold, many Californians also settled in Costa Rica and established coffee plantations when they found no gold. What is it about Californians, always looking for the quick buck? Like Australia, Costa Rica also became a dumping ground for foreign prisoners.

Next stop on our tour was Zoo Avenue. The zoo was a substitute for the Escalonia Cloud Forest Trail and Poas Volcano listed in our itinerary. About two weeks before we arrived, a 6.2 magnitude earthquake struck the Poas Volcano area. The January 2009 quake killed twenty-three people and closed the road leading to the volcano and trail. Instead, we visited a home for injured, donated, and confiscated animals and observed and photographed scarlet macaws, parrots, monkeys, toucans, raptors, pumas, turtles, and crocodiles. It was a good introduction to some of the wildlife later seen in the wild.

Like Wall Street fat cats obsessed with money, we traveled to downtown San Jose to visit the Gold and Numismatics (money) Museum. Along the way, we saw the ornate National Museum and Teatro Nacional (National Theater). One tour member spotted a pickpocket from the tour-bus window on the way to the museums.

Inside the museums, I learned that there were few Costa Rican gold deposits, just a little gold panning in the southwest. Pre-Columbian settlers used gold from other Central American countries to make intricate and beautifully crafted artifacts. Display artifacts included animals, jewelry, and burial items. Craftsmen melted gold in fires of one thousand degrees Fahrenheit or more and poured the molten gold into molds. They baked the clay molds in stone kilns and then broke off the mold to reveal gold artifacts. As a fused glass artist, Carol was intrigued by the kilns.

The money museum traced Costa Rica's history of paper and coin currency. When coffee-plantation owners wielded economic power, they paid workers in coffee beans honored as money only in plantation stores. Workers protested the unfair wage system, resulting in them receiving pay in official currency. They did not get paid "beans" anymore.

From the San Jose province, we motored to Braulio Carrillo National Park to experience its aerial tram. The park was one of fifty-seven parks in Heredia (city of flowers) province. To protect wildlife, the Costa Rican government banned hunting in 37 percent of the country's land base. Although we did not see much wildlife, we saw iron-gated and barbed-wired communities before entering the winding narrow roads of a cloud forest. Without local police departments, Costa Rican residents rely on private security systems to keep them safe from two-legged animals.

Like a small plane ascending to cruising altitude, we passed through a six-thousand-foot elevation cloud forest. We saw waterfalls cascading from the hillsides. Salmon-colored wild impatiens lined the roadside, and huge tree ferns that looked like palm trees covered the lush, steep hills. A broad-leafed rhubarb-looking plant called a poor man's umbrella dotted the landscape. We crossed the mustard-colored Sucio River to reach a magical forest with towering trees.

A naturalist led us on a short hike to the aerial-tram boarding area. I listened intently while swatting off pesky mosquitoes and avoiding leaf-carrying ants. The hour-and-a-half tram ride through the lower and upper rain forest canopies afforded us views of a chestnut-breasted mandible toucan; blue, yellow-black, and brown-white butterflies; and orchids. The rain forest was quiet, except for the constant buzz of the one-year cicada. Growing up in New Jersey, I was familiar with the sound of cicadas that only sang every seventeen years.

Peering down between our standing feet, we spotted the dark-green cow tongue leaf plant named for its shape and rough surface. After the tram ride, I saw my first Costa Rican wild snake. It was short and thin, yellow and green, and curled up on a small branch under a plant leaf.

For lunch, we stopped at a restaurant that had a salad bar and served rice and beans, squash, pork, beef, and chicken. I washed it down with a passion-fruit drink. Little did I know that twenty-four hours later, I would be sick from eating the restaurant's food. About a dozen Caravan tour group members shared my fate.

A kaleidoscope of color beckoned us after eating. Orange, black, white, blue, and gray butterflies fluttered around a screened-in garden. Cameras clicked when one paused long enough to strike a pose. A local boy picked up a poisonous red frog, rinsed its toxic secretions with water, and placed it on a large green leaf. Without shaking hands, we left the boy and frog to search for bananas.

With eyes peeled, our bus skidded to a stop at a Del Monte banana plantation. We watched men harvest ninety-pound bunches of green bananas and attach them to an overhead cable system. Once twenty-five bunches hung from the cables, several men pulled the half-ton banana train along a cable to an open shed. Then one man cut a bunch and removed the blue bag that protected the fruit from pesticides and herbicides. One such pest, the ferocious-looking rhinoceros beetle, is the largest scarab beetle, which was over two inches in length. This prehistoric creature lives in rotted wood or rich soil. A shaved ice vendor had one to show us, so our tour guide held it next to his open mouth while we took pictures.

Rhinoceros Beetle

About twenty-five workers moved, washed, cut, separated, weighed, and labeled smaller bunches of green bananas. They earned a monthly salary of $700 and free company housing. The forty-two-thousand-acre plantation annually produced four billion pounds of bananas. The United States bought about two-thirds of the production while Europe and other countries purchased the rest.

From the plantation, we passed a cattle ranch, where four cowboys on horses lassoed calves instead of bananas. Shortly thereafter, five black howler monkeys explored an oropendola nest in a tree.

To reach Tortuguero National Park, we traded our window sightseeing bus for a motorized riverboat cruise. On the river, we saw a tiger heron, egrets, a great egret, a roseate spoonbill, swallows, and a river otter.

Frommer's calls Tortuguero National Park the "Venice of Costa Rica" because of its maze of jungle canals that meander through a dense lowland rain forest. I likened it to the Amazon, because of its abundant wildlife. Our first morning in the park, I awoke to a symphony of animal sounds. *Hoot, hoot* went nature's alarm clock at 4:30 a.m. A half hour later, high-and low-pitched birds sounded throughout the jungle. A howler monkey chimed in with a low and loud growling noise that sounded like it came from a larynx-impaired throat, damaged by years of alcohol and nicotine abuse.

The loud and resonant sound of a howler travels about a mile. Biologists believe that howlers mark their territories with these deep guttural sounds. A boat guide explained that the howler near our lodge was banished from his group because he mated with the alpha male's girlfriend. Defeated and alone, our neighbor howler's call was wasted on the trees and tourists visiting Laguna Lodge.

Having an uncanny ability to mimic accents and other sounds, Carol echoed the howler's call and he responded. Their primal conversation lasted several minutes. Here's my feeble attempt to translate their conversation in Spanish:

Carol: Ola'. Mi llamo es Carol. Como se llamo?
Howler: Mi llamo es Freddie.
Carol: Como esta', Freddie?
Howler: Muy malo!
Carol: Porque?
Howler: Porque, no tengo amigos porque mi amigos no me gusta. El primero mono congo mi vence y ahora vivo solamente.
Carol: Povre cito!

Our attention turned to fellow travelers, who alerted us to baby green sea turtles scurrying on the beach. I was excited and surprised to find several newly hatched babies breaststroking in the sand. January was outside the *tortuguera negra* (green turtle) nesting season, so I was resigned to missing this blessed event. I was pleasantly surprised to witness the longest-living reptiles embark on their annual migration to Florida and Caribbean beaches. One of the river guides speculated that the lodge lights attracted a few female turtles to lay their eggs early. The turtles are very sensitive to light, and locals warned us not to use camera flashes when photographing them.

Worldwide, six of seven sea turtle species are listed as endangered, and some populations are critically close to extinction. Sea turtles first arrived in Costa Rica in 1592. Due to over harvesting of eggs, sea turtles faced extinction in the 1950s. The Costa Rican government regulated harvesting in 1963 and established Tortuguero National Park in 1970 to give them additional protection. Four different sea turtles nest in the park: (1) green, (2) hawksbill, (3) loggerhead, and (4) giant leatherbacks. Green turtles are the most common.

The baby turtles seemed disoriented. Some headed to the pool while others moved into the jungle. Well-intentioned tourists picked up the wayward babies and pointed them toward the ocean. Like paparazzi stalking Hollywood celebrities, several photographers digitally recreated the turtles' every move until foamy surf launched them on their nautical voyage.

All of this excitement before breakfast whetted our appetites for food. We headed to the buffet area when we saw a nest of Montezuma oropendolas. Oropendolas are birds with red beaks, yellow tails, black heads, and brown bodies. Their elongated brown nest, made of interwoven sticks, stems, and grasses, hung from the tree branches like a giant teardrop. Hanging upside down like bats on steroids, the birds emitted loud calls.

Like sea turtles out of water, life-vested torsos with flailing arms and legs boarded riverboats, along with naturalist guides and drivers. Our guide's name was Franklin, and he spoke English with a strong Jamaican accent. The sun reflected off this pirate's gold tooth as he talked at length about the mating practices of turtles and monkeys. Turtles are monogamous while monkeys mate with more than one partner. He said that male turtle erections last so long that a female turtle has to work at dislodging the mounted male after hours of copulation. Franklin swore that "turtle prick dust," when rubbed on a man's penis, ensured an erection that lasted two hours. Since the dominant male howler monkey mates with all of the females in his territory, I wondered if he had a source for "prick dust" in the turtle community.

While howler monkeys are herbivores, spider monkeys are omnivores. White-faced capuchin monkeys are very intelligent and can be trained to be many things: cosmonaut, waiters, service animals for the handicapped, musicians, and pickpockets. And you thought you were irreplaceable?

We saw all three monkey species on our Tortuguero canal tours. In addition, I photographed the following wildlife: (1) yellow-crowned night heron, (2) belted kingfisher, (3) mud and black river turtles, (4) walking Jesus green lizard, (5) brown, orange, grey, and green iguanas, (6) caiman, (7) northern jacana, and (8) an anhinga (feminist bird of Costa Rica).

After the second boat tour of the day, I returned to my room feeling sick, achy, tired, queasy, and feverish. I heard about another tour member getting sick earlier in the day and wondered if we shared the same malady. I skipped dinner that night and went to bed instead. Sleep eluded me, as diarrhea kept me in the bathroom most of the night. Despite the high room temperature and humidity, I felt chilled and wrapped my body in extra blankets to keep warm.

I knew I did not have malaria, because I had taken vitamin B1 and prescribed pills prior to the trip. Could I have dengue fever, I wondered. My wife, a registered nurse and previous traveler to Central America, diagnosed it as *tourist trots / Montezuma's revenge,* otherwise known as dysentery or food poisoning.

Sleep deprived and with no appetite, I sat on the porch for some fresh air as my wife walked to breakfast. A woman from the adjoining room also skipped breakfast and rocked on her porch chair. We talked. She also was sick and joked that "we taxed the lodge's septic system last night." I laughed and said, "Misery likes company." She said that two other people were sick, and for the rest of the trip, we compared notes on the daily "body count." Once back in the United States, she e-mailed me her doctor's diagnosis of salmonella and E. coli contamination.

Bless her heart and head, Carol packed Imodium, ibuprofen, and Cipro antibiotic; so I was one of the lucky ones who recovered quickly. I felt well enough to go to the Green Turtle Research Station and learn about its efforts to protect the turtle's nesting habitat, eggs, and young hatchlings. Next, we toured Tortuguero village to shop and people watch. I especially enjoyed the little children playing ball in the middle of the main street. The faces of some older Jamaicans also caught my eye. I asked one waitress if I could take her picture, and she shyly nodded yes.

Rather than walk from the village back to the lodge, Carol and I took the boat. Three women who hiked back got quite a surprise. While they stopped to chat, a reptilian rope slithered around one woman's ankle. Oblivious to the snake that climbed halfway to her knee, her companions saw it and yelled. With a British-accented scream and a swift leg kick, she dislodged the snake. One of her companions joked, "It was the most tactile action she had gotten on the trip."

The sun shone brightly on day five as the healthy and the sick boarded our riverboat to return to civilization. Like a Joseph Conrad character in the *Heart of Darkness*, I battled a jungle sickness and survived. Too weak to hold a camera, I watched the other photographers with their electronic appendages scan and record the fleeting jungle sights. Like the third eye celebrated in several Asian cultures, they captured sights blind to the naked eye.

Our jungle cruise completed, we emptied our bladders before boarding our bus. The daily body count was up to six, so our tour director promised to stop at a *farmicia* (drug store) on our way to Fortuna. He said that six members from another Caravan tour group had also fallen ill. Sick spouses found single bus seats to limit contagion while Tony distributed plastic barf bags for the nauseous.

The scenic countryside through the San Carlos Valley lifted my spirits, but the winding narrow roads and bridges bothered my stomach. Our lunch stop was a feast for the eyes. Four senoritas dressed like Carmen Miranda danced while we ate. To the beat of Calypso music, these curvaceous cuties cavorted. Like howler monkeys on the make, the male photographers quickly left their lunch plates (and spouses) to get a better view of the shapely bronzed bodies. After strolling along a river and garden near the restaurant, I returned to the bus with my physical and artistic appetites satiated.

The long and winding road ended at the Arenal Manoa Hotel, where the staff greeted us with complimentary cocktails and room keys. As the sun set, we walked to our spacious rooms while bellboys went door-to-door delivering luggage.

The private duplex units had high wood-beamed ceilings with beautiful landscaping along the patio and entry door. Unfortunately, it was a cloudy night, so we couldn't see Arenal Volcano's nightly lava show. One couple, who took a small van ride closer to the volcano, said it was not worth the trip because of the scary and bumpy ride and poor visibility.

The next morning (day six), we awoke to pouring rain. Carol and I skipped the boat cruise through Cano Negro Wildlife Refuge because I was still sick, and neither of us wanted to endure another long bus ride. Those who went on the tour saw a sloth and a red monkey with a baby. I was jealous when I saw their pictures.

Instead, we relaxed at the hotel and walked around the manicured hotel grounds, which overlooked a working farm, river, and pond. A Magnificent Owl butterfly sitting next to a red, yellow, and green heliconia plant greeted us when we returned to our room. Afraid to drink the tap water in our hotel room, we filled up a backpack water bladder at the lodge restaurant. The Spanish-speaking staff had never seen such a water carrier, and it took a small committee to figure out how to fill it. It was all rather amusing.

Magnificent Owl Butterfly

Day seven was partly sunny as we boarded our bus to the Hanging Bridges trail near Arenal Volcano. Soon after leaving the hotel, the driver stopped so we could take pictures of several raccoonlike creatures called white-faced coati. A car with environmentally impaired locals stopped to feed the wild animals. In a flash, a dozen or more coati appeared and enjoyed a feeding frenzy that blocked traffic. After our driver scolded the locals, the crowd dispersed, and we continued our journey.

More wildlife appeared as we drove around Arenal Lake. We spotted a crested guan that looked like a black vulture with a red neck flap. A Great Kiskadee with yellow breast, brown wings, and black-and-white striped head appeared out the window. We saw commercial tilapia fish farms on the lake's shores, and our guide said private anglers catch tilapia that escape from the farms. Before fish farms, sugarcane was the major economic mainstay of the town of Canas. I also read the lake provided habitat for windsurfers, although I did not see any during our drive.

Midmorning, we arrived at the Hanging Gardens trail. Carol and I joined the group opting for the guided two-mile hike over six suspension bridges. The loop trail through the lush tropical canopy took nearly two hours and included a three-hundred-foot elevation gain. We saw waterfalls and views of a steaming Mount Arenal.

For lunch, we ate at a restaurant cooperative that donated proceeds to local schools. Tired of chicken, it was nice to see fresh fish (sea bass) on the menu. Local children sold chocolate-covered coffee beans for dessert. After lunch, we motored through the province of Guanacaste, named after Costa Rica's national tree. Translated into Spanish, "Guanacaste" means "tree of ears," descriptive of the shape of its seed pods. We saw several such trees as we traveled through the tropical dry forests of the Guanacaste province. Other trees along the road included purple jacaranda, orange flame of the forest, scarlet poro, and ash.

As we neared the Pan-American Highway on our way to the Dona Ana Beach Hotel, we passed a people plantation (cemetery). There are many cemeteries in Costa Rica because the people do not believe in cremation. They bury the body whole so "God doesn't have to put together so many pieces," according to our tour director.

Tony added that Costa Ricans preferred burial to make it easy for God. Costa Ricans are concerned that God may mix up the puzzle pieces and make a saint out of a sinner. I felt the discussion ironic since I had packed my parent's ashes. That night, toasting the sunset overlooking the Golfo de Nicoya, Carol and I discussed spreading my parents' ashes along the beach next to our hotel. My parents had shared seven days of our adventure, and it was time to lighten our load to make room for souvenirs. I said good-bye to their bodies at their funerals in 2007 and 2008, but now was the time to say good-bye to their spirits.

A blue cloudless sky greeted us the next morning. We ate breakfast before walking to the beach. The hotel security guards advised against bringing valuables and made us sign a liability waiver since hotel security did not patrol the entire beach. I left my camera behind and carried two plastic boxes containing my parents' ashes. Once alone,

Carol and I spoke to my parents, and I poured their cremated remains in the water. I felt unburdened and knew my parents approved of their final resting place.

The rest of the day, we celebrated life with tropical drinks, salsa lessons, water aerobics, and lots of food. That night, at around 8:00 p.m., we heard loud explosions outside our room. It scared us half to death. I thought the noise sounded like gunshots, so I was a little nervous, especially after talking to security earlier that day. I was relieved to learn that party fireworks, and not guns, were responsible.

Day nine meant it was time to hop on the bus and head back to San Jose for our last hotel stay and farewell dinner. We stopped in Sarica for lunch and watched Costa Rica's version of *Dancing with the Stars*. A blue-and-white-clad male and female dance team twisted, twirled, and turned around the dance floor. His white pants and her dress matched their bright smiles. Their blue tops shimmered as they moved to the bolero and meringue rhythms. Columbia-style red-and-white outfits followed as they danced to a country song. Turquoise costumes framed muscular bodies entwined in a tango beat. Carol joined the male dancer as he gave salsa lessons to several ladies. We all had a good laugh.

After lunch, we stopped at Grecia to see a metal church built in the 1890s. Assembled in Belgium and shipped to Costa Rica in pieces, European settlers from Italy, Netherlands, and Greece reassembled the church in Grecia. They chose metal for the church to avoid damage from earthquakes. The town was also famous for its colorful wooden oxcarts that celebrated the transportation role oxcarts played before the railroad.

Outside Grecia, we passed sugarcane fields. We saw workers cut the sugarcane, bundle it, and ship it by truck to the Grecia sugarcane mill. Next, we passed the Guaro rum distillery, and I remembered my head swimming after sampling the potent rum elsewhere.

Our last stop before the hotel was the Britt Coffee Plant in Heredia province. Arabica coffee beans thrive in Costa Rica's volcanic soil and mountainous regions. Workers hand harvest the red-colored beans in summer. Next, they dry the beans and peel them to obtain the seed. Nothing is wasted, as beans are roasted for coffee. Workers recycle peels and plant the white seeds in the soil. Once a seed is planted, it takes three months for a leaf to appear. Workers add chicken manure to the soil, and a new coffee plant is ready in a year.

Actors led us into a comfortable theater, where we watched a spirited play about the history of coffee and Britt's coffee production process. Through film clips, stage props, and costumed actors, we learned where coffee was first discovered, how it was introduced to Costa Rica, and Britt's roasting and packaging processes. Audience volunteers depicted the tasting and smelling process used "to break a cup" of coffee. After tasting their coffee, I brought some home and later purchased some online.

Live piano music accompanied our farewell dinner and after-dinner group photograph. Amidst rumors of a taxi strike, we retired to our rooms and slept until breakfast. To our relief, we did not experience any transportation problems until we got to the airport. There, we waited in line for an hour to check our bags to Portland, Oregon. Once on the plane, take-off was delayed until strong winds calmed.

I sat in the rear of the plane next to two members of the Costa Rican Special Olympics floor hockey team. They were going to Boise, Idaho, to participate in the 2009 Winter Special Olympics Game. Their names were Ary and Mario, and I shared my chocolate-covered fruit with them. Since I sat in the window seat, Ary asked me to take pictures with his camera. I even got a tip (in Costa Rican currency) for my assistance.

Once in the air, I was glad to have a window seat on such a clear day. Lake Nicaragua gleamed below us and surrounded two cloud-capped volcanoes. The craters, filled with cotton-ball clouds, cried for further exploration. Our flight path followed the coastlines of El Salvador and Guatemala. Dark-and light-green farm parcels dotted the landscape like mosaic tiles. Four cinder cone volcanoes lined up like guard towers protecting the natural wonders that lie beyond.

We passed white-sand beaches as the plane veered over Mexico. The landscape patches seen through cloud breaks reminded me of the limestone walls of Yucatan Peninsula *cenotes*. "I Dreamed There Was No War" played through my headphones as the clear air turbulence and free red wine rocked me to sleep. The captain's voice woke me and pointed out Mexico City and several tall volcanoes.

Brown, barren, and flat described the landscape north of Mexico City. A few puffs of clouds cast shadows that looked like lakes. Parquet floor patterns of empty land radiated from urban centers while roads and highways looked like spokes on a wagon wheel. Closer to the United

States border, the light-brown soil turned red. Was this symbolic of the blood shed by Mexicans searching for freedom or just a change in rock color? Small towns in gridlike patterns stood out like floor drains in a shower, unable to rinse the land stained by Hispanic corpses.

The closer we got to the American border town of Nogales, Texas, the clouds and air turned dirtier, like the political winds that stoke the flames of racial intolerance. The haze cleared to reveal rugged mountains, which resembled the spine of a gray iguana. These mountains dwarfed the white concrete border fence in height and splendor, as do many of God's creations when compared to human monuments to fear and hate. A large body of brown water flanked the western side of the mountain range while greener, clearer lake water appeared further east. American settlements were few and far between, protected, I assumed, by armed vigilantes with orders to shoot to kill.

A long river snaked its way through the adobe-colored topography and joined a green lake. Tan mesas and river valleys gave way to higher and darker gray hills and mountains. Deep gorges extended their liquid ribbons toward a desert city. Smoother black landforms snaked through the landscape like cooled lava. Wispy cloud bands streamed like jet contrails dispersed by the wind.

Layers of transparent clouds rushed over dry ground once underwater. Denser clouds blocked my view until tall, jagged mountain peaks poked through like shark fins in the ocean. Jade-colored squares marked the floor of a fertile valley connected to another green square by a serpentine waterway.

A long, narrow, and irregular coastline outlined an emerald-colored lake. Surface mining dotted the hillsides above the lake, exposing yellow and rust-hued mineral deposits. An open-pit mine revealed layers of igneous, metamorphic, and sedimentary rocks colored red, green, and tan. A mountain, worthy of the Cascades, loomed in the distance, and to the south, an area of volcanic wasteland reminded me of Mount St. Helens.

As we descended into the Tucson/Phoenix area, residential developments resembled clogged arteries flowing through sun-bleached corpses. If I were an undocumented worker, I would head for the green sustainable life of Costa Rica, rather than to a state on life support from the Colorado River.

After visiting Costa Rica, I understood why a young soldier would give up his life for his country. It is a nation of underdogs symbolized by the Special Olympics floor hockey team who battled in Boise, the persecuted and prosecuted immigrants that settled its shores, and the Britt Coffee Company employees who helped poor villagers rebuild after a severe earthquake;a culture that embraced peace, not police; environment, not envy; and education, not eradication. Sustained by nature's bounty and beauty, Costa Rica's *pura vida* (for life) mantra mended hearts and souls wearied by war and death.

Chapter Ten

"Philadelphia Freedom"

Swinging in the shadows of New York and Chicago, America's Liberty Bell rang loudly from the City of Brotherly Love and former US capitol. Walking its streets, I was reminded of the historic role Philadelphia played in the founding of our country and the formation of its governing ideals. All streets led to freedom in this well-planned river city-from the cobbled stone streets near Independence Hall to the park-like Penn campus where Ben Franklin's statue reminds students of the freedom and equality born from access to public education.

Freedom of religion rang from the diverse houses of worship and celebrated the tolerance that allowed blacks, Quakers, Jews, Catholics, and Protestants to live and pray side by side. US public higher education and the freedom it brings started with the establishment of the University of Pennsylvania. Philadelphia's educational legacy continued with Drexel and Temple universities. Public spaces like Washington Park and Rittenhouse Square, with their historic statues and colorful fall foliage, reminded me of the freedom of urban parks and public discourse that's needed in crowded cities. Lastly, freedom rang from Philly's stop on the Underground Railroad, where slaves escaped the tyranny of plantation life.

But it was freedom of expression that brought my wife and I to the banks of the Schulkill River in October 2009, to enjoy our son acting in the play *History Boys*. The Arden Theater, one of Philadelphia's thriving playhouses, cast him as Lockwood, whose thrift-store fashion defined a funky character. His love of history inspired him to follow a heroic military career. The play was set in the 1980s, in a northern England high school, where eight lads studied for final examinations that determined whether their dreams of attending Oxford or Cambridge were realized.

One critic who reviewed the play thought it relevant to American students striving for an Ivy League education. I could identify with that critic as a product of an all-boys college preparatory high school and successful graduate of an Ivy League school. I liked the play's humor and its topical treatment of an American educational issue, involving teaching for test results versus teaching students to think creatively. Regardless of how history is taught, the play demonstrated the wisdom of the quote, "Those who don't know history are bound to repeat its mistakes."

In a culture that worships youth and living in the now, Philadelphia deifies the past. Its narrow streets, tree-lined row houses, and national historical parks are shrines to America's beginnings and memorials to our country's Founding Fathers. Betsy Ross House is the city's token celebration of a "founding female." As Dorothy Lintott's character in the *History Boys* stated, "What is history? History is women following behind men with buckets."

Besides my son's debut in Philadelphia's theater circles, I discovered that Philly's culinary delights extended beyond cheesesteaks and Tastykakes. Both Thai and Irish restaurants we tried were excellent. New buildings around Penn and construction on the city's convention center showed progress, as did a musical venue called World Cafe. Borrowing an idea from other US river cities, Philadelphia developed a paved running, walking, and cycling path along what used to be called the Sure Kill River because of its pollution. Our walk along this path found stagnant water but awesome reflections on a sunny day.

My sunny disposition turned cloudy, as I discovered a bench on the Penn campus, located between the Van Pelt Library and my Alpha Chi Rho fraternity house. Inscribed on a metal plate fastened to the wooden bench were the words "In Memory of Mitchell Todd Morris, C'73." Mitchell was one of my college roommates during my freshman and sophomore years at Penn. When Mitchell and I double-dated in college, his girlfriend's name was Alice, and my girlfriend's name was Carol.

Using Mitch's middle name for introductions, we referred to ourselves as Bob, Carol, Todd, and Alice, after a movie of a similar title.

Any city that claims Bill Cosby as a native son must have a sense of humor. We found it when we toured my old Penn fraternity house, Alpha Chi Rho (AXP). I rang the front doorbell, and one of my "Crow House" brothers let us in. The first thing my son noticed was the huge moose head hanging over the living room fireplace. Our tour guide explained that the animal trophy was not the original fraternity moose head that graced the mantle during my college days, 1969–1973. He said that AXP got a new moose head in 2001, after another fraternity stole the original trophy and chained it to its living room wall.

Pennsylvania is coal country, and Philadelphia pays homage to that fossil fuel with its coal-fired pizza ovens. Unlike West Coast wood-fired ovens that provide extra fiber and a smooth smoky aroma, I can only imagine that a coal-fired pizza oven caused black-lung disease and left many carbon prints.

But in that season's scare from the H1N1 swine flu virus, coal-fired ovens were the least of our travel worries. My wife packed extra masks to ward off germs and even offered one to a sneezing plane passenger. After shaking someone's hand, I always squirted some antiseptic gel on my hands. I referred to this policy as "Trust but Sterilize."

Phillies Phever gripped the city as fans awaited the start of the upcoming World Series with the New York Yankees. Bus electronic reader boards flashed "GO PHILLIES," and storefront windows had spiderwebs that spelled out the same sentiment. Green foam fingers, red-and-white T-shirts, and fan signs were everywhere at a noontime city hall rally. One athletic fan climbed a public statue and pulled a Phillies T-shirt over a small bronzed child held by its mother.

This trip was my first look at the outside of the Constitution museum that anchored one end of Independence Mall. At the other end sat Independence Hall, where the Declaration of Independence was signed on July 4, 1776. The preamble to the Constitution was etched on the outside of the Constitution museum.

The historical quote reminded me of a class discussion I had with junior high students about the natural rights guaranteed to all Americans by the US Constitution and Declaration of Independence. One eighth grader astutely commented that undocumented workers should have these natural rights too since neither historical document differentiates between Americans and American citizens.

Our son was such a success in *History Boys* that the Arden Theater offered him the lead role in *Peter Pan.* That meant that Carol and I returned to Philadelphia in late December 2009 to cheer on our talented son. We also celebrated my fifty-eighth birthday and New Year's during our return visit.

A mummer is a person who wears a fantastic mask or disguise usually to celebrate Christmas or New Year's. Mummery is as old as the imagination. Its history traces from pagan Rome and ancient Greece to Europe and Russia. Mummers search for excuses to revel. Some agricultural societies celebrated harvest with festivals marked by parades and displays of fanciful costumes. On December 17, Romans celebrated the ancient god of agriculture, Saturn, with unrestrained merrymaking. In Christian cultures of North and South America, people celebrate Mardi Gras and carnival parades to mark the beginning of the Lenten fast.

Dating to the 1700s, the annual New Year's Day Mummers Parade in Philadelphia continues this rich tradition of family and tourist-friendly drunken stupor in hopes of driving out the evil spirits of the past and welcoming the good *spirits* of the New Year (pun intended). Community groups, representing different city neighborhoods, march from Washington and Broad streets to city hall in kaleidoscopic costumes, with cacophonous bands, and in psychedelic floats. Thousands of spectators lined city sidewalks from 10:00 a.m. to dusk to watch, wave, applaud, dance, and laugh at the free entertainment.

The dudes and wenches were the first performers we saw at the corner of Pine and Broad. Two dudes unloaded free cans of beer from the back of a white delivery truck like foreign aid workers at a natural disaster. Many revelers and parade watchers, with their red eyes and flushed faces, looked hungover. The only wenches I saw were two guys dressed as female cheerleaders, holding a banner with a cartoon picture of "Rush Limblah" dressed in a red skirt and yellow sweater, holding a black megaphone. The words "blah, blah, blah, blah" floated from Rush's mouth like stale champagne bubbles. One side of the banner carried the words "cheer" and "drill club," and the other side had the phone number 1-800-HATE-YOU.

One cheerleader with heavily red-rouged cheeks wore a yellow sweatshirt with a large letter *L* on his chest, framed by platinum blond strands of hair. He also wore a light-green pleated skirt with yellow socks. His golden pom-poms matched his gold spray-painted shoes and reflected one of the parade's signature band tunes, "Oh Dem Golden Slippers".

Another cross-dressing cheerleader wore a gray wig and ermine scarf draped across the front of her V-necked, reddish-orange dress. Covering "trannies" upper back was a red, orange, and black suitcase with a sign that read BAGS FLY FREE. He flashed one photographer with a wrinkled and saggy boob and, from his rear, mooned onlookers with shiny plastic buttocks.

The clowns followed the more traditional mummers, who wore feathers like a peacock. One red and white-faced clown wore a sparkly silver, orange, pink, and beige suit, with a matching orange crown. He looked more like a devil than a clown, engulfed by red and orange feathers that looked like hellfire. I guessed he was one of the bad spirits.

To combat that evil spirit, an attractive black-haired woman pulled a wheeled altar draped in a multicolored blanket of green, blue, and purple satin fabric, fringed with pink and gold. On top of the altar was a pink fringed circle with concentric circles, the color of rainbows. Like rays from the sun, white feathers embroidered in red, gold, green, and blue and dappled with white cotton balls encircled the pink sphere. I wondered if this float symbolized the feminine side of Christ popularized by *The Da Vinci Code*. Could the pink host and its rainbow coalition be like the symbolic body of Christ held high during the benediction of the Holy Eucharist? Or was this an endorsement of female and homosexual priests?

A more secular good spirit, straight out of Disney's *Aladdin* movie, emerged from a large golden lamp, followed by a float shaped like a chicken. To celebrate the good fall harvest, a farmer in blue coveralls accompanied the chicken float, walking two fake chickens on a wire harness attached to his body. A few clips of a wire cutter, and he could have roasted those birds rotisserie style. A large orange and black butterfly, with wings that looked like stained glass, fluttered while chased by an enormous bluish-silver dragon with red eyes, metallic-blue head, gold teeth, and purple and white wings. His scaly talons grasped a purple velvet cushion, carrying a golden crown. Was this a dragon from the King Arthur legend or a dragon from Harry Potter books?

After two hours of eye candy, I was ready for ear sweets. Tambourines, banjos, saxophones, snare and bass drums, accordions, and trombones filled my ears with music that lifted my spirits and moved my body parts in time to the rhythmic melodies. Musicians dressed as flowers, fruits, and felines filled the chilly air with sounds that warmed the body and the soul.

Walking down the sidewalk dressed in my new yellow L.L. Bean rain gear and gray goatee, I looked like a fisherman prepared for the perfect storm. In fact, I heard a few comments about the "big blow" coming, but I was determined to show off my wife's Christmas present and stay dry. Suddenly, I was grabbed by the shoulders and was boozily asked if I would pose for a picture with two male partygoers. Evidently, they thought my *Rime of the Ancient Mariner* costume was more interesting than the mummers. In a spirit of brotherly love, I smiled, flashed two thumbs up, and posed with two new friends.

New Year's Eve is usually anticlimactic for me since it is the day after my birthday. My wife and I usually celebrate it with champagne and the remote control. I have youthful memories of trying to get last-minute dates for New Year's Eve parties. Older and hopefully wiser, I am wary of sharing the road with drunken drivers. But this New Year's Eve was special, because I spent it in Philadelphia surrounded by my wife and grown children. After sharing presents, eggnog, and cider, we walked to an Irish restaurant for New Year's Eve dinner. As unexpected fireworks lit up the dark sky, I hummed Jimmy Buffet's song, "The Night I Painted the Sky."

For my fifty-eighth birthday, my daughter and I visited the National Constitution Museum. Its award-winning and acclaimed multimedia production was worth the price of admission. Sitting in a circular theatre, listening to an impassioned African American female narrate the history of the US Constitution was like watching a one-person Broadway play. I felt like I was in the US Senate chambers, listening to an eloquent speaker describe how the Constitution, although written in 1787, was not a brittle piece of history, but rather, as current as the issues (e.g., abortion, immigration) of our day. She explained how the document, a replica of which was on exhibit, was about our rights and responsibilities.

It was hard not to be reminded about our constitutional rights while touring the museum. The words that guarantee those rights, starting with the phrase, "We, the people, hold these truths self evident that all men are created equal and endowed with certain inalienable rights to life, liberty, and the pursuit of happiness," literally jumped out from the museum walls. However, understanding the individual responsibilities that accompany these rights took more work.

As I stood with one hand on the Bible and another raised upward, I recited the oath that all foreign nationals must recite before they are granted US citizenship. I recommend that all Americans, young and old, do this as a civics course refresher. The oath reminds newly nationalized citizens that the rights granted to them come with responsibilities to support the common good through military or other public service. Naturally born US citizens should have these same responsibilities.

The museum's brochure estimates an hour to tour the building. However, my daughter and I stayed there for two hours and hardly scratched the surface. There were several cyclonic-looking towers of video screens allowing easy electronic access to information about famous Americans. For those with big egos and dreams, you could pretend to take the presidential oath in front of a video screen showing cheering fans and even replay the historic moment.

Most fascinating was the Hall of Signers. Life-sized bronze statues of thirty-nine constitutional convention delegates (and three dissenters), who signed the Constitution, appeared in various poses. Each statue had a bronze plaque that identified names, ages, and geographic residences. It was a great place for pictures.

Another birthday wish was to have Philadelphia cheesesteaks for dinner and Tastykakes for dessert. Rachel, Christopher, and I met at a crowded South Street restaurant and waited in a line that spilled out to the sidewalk, like melted cheese off a greasy hoagie roll. Arriving early, Christopher held our place in line while Rachel and I barged through hungry traffic.

The smell of grilled beef, provolone cheese, onions, and peppers motivated our every step. The chef, who took my order, looked like a linebacker for the Eagles. I said, "Cheesesteak with provolone and peppers for here," and in no time, I had my birthday meal. When the cashier learned I was a Capricorn, she gave me a free beer and said,

"Us Capricorns gotta stick together, honey." For an added bonus, my son picked up the check.

It was appropriate that Carol and I came to Philadelphia to see our son perform in a play about history. Philadelphia was where we met, fell in love, and grew emotionally and intellectually. Like going to a wedding, the trip had something old (history), something new (Constitution museum), something borrowed (waterfront recreation), and something blue (the death of a Penn classmate).

Chapter Eleven

"Aeroplane"

We followed the Cape Air gate attendant to the twin-prop Cessna aircraft as the sun was setting in San Juan, Puerto Rico. The young pilot put down his newspaper as he welcomed us aboard and assigned seats. Carol elbowed me and nervously shared her concern about a newspaper-reading pilot who was not doing any "pilot things," like checking gauges and talking to the tower. Having flown with several Alaskan bush pilots, I was less nervous.

One older passenger rode in the cockpit seat, next to the captain, as his wife took the seat behind the pilot. Carol and I sat in the third row, both of us assigned window and aisle seats on either side of the plane. One advantage of single-engine commuter aircraft is there are no middle seats. Three other passengers took seats in the back of the plane, next to baggage too big to fit in the wings or nose. When one passenger jokingly asked if there was a movie on the flight, the pilot answered, "Just look out the windows."

Noise from the engines made it impossible to talk, so Carol slept while I gazed out the windows on our way to St. Croix, Virgin Islands. Flying below the clouds, the lights of Puerto Rico faded as darkened landforms and waterways guided us to our destination. Instead of worrying I was flying *Cape Fear* airlines, I glanced toward the cockpit, aglow with white-lighted dials, gauges, and switches, curious but confident our pilot knew what he was doing. My confidence turned to excitement as the pilot headed the nose of the plane toward the runway lights of Christiansted, St. Croix Airport and gently touched down on the smooth asphalt runway.

After walking along a serpentine pathway through a neatly tended garden, our smiling host, originally from Guyana, showed us in to his bed-and-breakfast. We walked passed colorfully padded wicker chairs and a sofa next to an Internet-connected laptop computer. On the left, we passed the roomy kitchen and breakfast area. Through an open courtyard with an aquamarine-tiled freshwater pool, we headed to our periwinkle-colored room and patio overlooking Christiansted Harbor. Marine life inspired paintings adorned our room and adjoining recreation area.

The first night, we slept well, exhausted from our eighteen-hour journey from Oregon but soothed by Caribbean breezes. The saltwater-scented air was aromatherapy for me as it filtered through billowing curtains. Morning sunlight caressed us awake more gently than our white light machine in Oregon City.

Dollar-sized pancakes, covered in blueberry syrup, sausages, and local fruit, filled our plate as if painted on by a culinary artist with a spatula rather than a paintbrush. My wife enjoyed the tea selection, but the high-test coffee was too weak for my tastes. Fruit juices and breads rounded out the menu.

Ignoring our hosts' safety warnings about traffic and no sidewalks, we walked to town on a mile of dirt-road shoulders, admiring trees, flowers, and old churches. A short older woman with a strong New England accent welcomed us to the NPS's cramped visitor center. She quickly gave us NPS brochures, local bus schedules, and information on boat/snorkeling tours to Buck Island National Monument.

We spent several hours walking around the Christiansted fort, town, and waterfront. Seeking islands on which to cultivate sugar and expand trading partners, the Danish West India and Guinea Company explored St. John, St. Thomas, and St. Croix from 1672 to 1733. Because St. Croix was flatter, larger, and more fertile, the company purchased St. Croix. For their first settlement, the Danes chose a good harbor on the northeast coast, the site of an earlier French village. Their leader named the settlement Christiansted in honor of reigning King Christian VI and surveyed the island into 150-acre plantations.

As St. Croix's sugarcane and rum economy grew, population increased to ten thousand, including nine thousand West African slaves.

St. Croix became the capital of the "Danish Islands in America." Many planters, merchants, and traders reaped great profits, as reflected in the fine architecture of the town and country. To protect its investment from pirates, privateers, slave uprisings, and other European countries, the Danes built Fort Christiansted between 1749 and 1841.

The fort was armed with six and eighteen-pounder cannons. These guns and two outlying batteries, combined with a formidable reef, dominated the harbor entrance. In 1830, Christiansted's garrison numbered 215 officers and men, including a corps of musicians. Slaves given freedom for faithful service or for money earned as artisans and farmers manned the fire brigade. Other free blacks worked as small merchants, fishermen, seamen, shoemakers, tailors, masons, carpenters, and blacksmiths. To distinguish themselves from slaves, free black men wore a red and white ornament on their hats.

After walking around the fort, we strolled along the waterfront, checking out restaurant menus. Then we browsed stores along narrow cobblestone streets, looking for deals on T-shirts and other souvenirs. Hot from the humidity and still recovering from our long flight, we decided not to walk back to our lodging. Thirty long minutes after the scheduled departure time for a local bus, we decided to take a taxi. Expecting to hear some tourist information, our salt and pepper-haired driver ranted about having to pay higher costs for a vehicle license and maintenance. Much to my amusement and entertainment, his loud banter continued until we arrived back to our bed and breakfast.

Thanks to a 150-proof Cruzan rum, we slept through the noisy partying and smelly smoking of our Canadian cohabitants. Over a breakfast of scrambled eggs and cheese, sausages, fruit, and toast, we found out that another couple staying in our B and B was going on the same sailing and snorkeling tour to Buck Island. However, our attempts to share a taxi with them foundered, because the honeymooners were late to breakfast.

The 127-acre uninhabited Buck Island National Monument rose 328 feet above sea level and was located one and a half miles off the northeast side of St. Croix. It was surrounded by an 18,839 acre submerged land and coral reef system. In 1989, Hurricane Hugo decimated a large portion of Buck Island's coral ecosystem, which is still threatened by overfishing, climate change, pollution, sedimentation, and boat damage. To preserve one of the finest marine gardens in the Caribbean Sea, the

NPS limited access to protect endangered and threatened species living and nesting there. Daily concessioners offered full and half-day boat tours for snorkeling and other activities.

Carol and I sat on the bow underneath a large sail with a picture of the tour's owner, Bob (Big Beard). We gazed upon the sparkly bright water surface for signs of humpback whales and dolphins seen the previous day. Failing to spot any marine mammals, I directed my attention to the bikini-clad first mate while Carol stared at the charismatic blond second mate, who looked like a cross between Tom Petty, the musician, and Dirk Nowitzki, the Dallas Mavericks' star basketball player.

We landed briefly on Buck Island to try on snorkeling equipment and get acclimated to the water conditions. The only hiking trail on the island was closed for repairs, so access was limited to the beach area. The captain blew into a huge conch shell, and its siren song signaled it was time to board and sail to the underwater snorkeling trail.

I felt like Jacques Cousteau sailing around Buck Island. Patches of deeper dark and light-blue water, interspersed among shallow turquoise pools, mesmerized. The calm and clear Caribbean water contrasted with the rough brown rocks and cactus lining the tropical dry Buck Island landscape. Underwater, the stark brown and white elk horn coral clashed with the bright silver barracuda and blue tangs.

Lunch at a private St. Croix beach was like a scene from the movie *Cast Away* or the television show *Gilligan's Island*. A tattered canvas sail provided shade over plywood benches and a table while a water cooler filled with rum punch provided refreshment. For entertainment, we chatted, watched the captain grill lunch, and laughed as pesky mongoose begged for handouts. St. Croix inhabitants introduced mongoose to the island to eat rats. Like many invasive species, the mongoose overpopulated and started eating endangered sea turtle eggs.

Returning to the Christiansted waterfront, we shopped and ate dinner at Angry Nates. I forgot to ask the waitress why Nate was angry. While dining, a charter fishing boat arrived and its crew unloaded several mahimahi and barracuda, stiff from rigor mortis. The water next to the docked boat boiled with the fins and tails of hungry tarpon, fighting for the entrails from the gutted fish.

The next day we found out how difficult it was to rent a car at the last minute. While the rental car companies blamed the shortage of cars on the busy winter 2010 tourist season, others blamed it on Toyota's accelerator recall and oil refinery maintenance. Undaunted, a taxi took us to Cane Bay for snorkeling and hiking. With rented fins and personal masks and snorkels, we swam toward the Great Wall, where water depths plunged to over three thousand feet. Unable to reach our destination, we turned back after swimming to an anchored dive ship. Returning to shore, we passed a mature green sea turtle, tangs, wrasse, and a school of squid. The view of barrel and brain coral was marred by a car floor mat and golf ball on the sandy bottom.

Swimming with the Turtle

Lured by tales of magnificent tide pools, we walked two miles along North Shore Road to the beautifully landscaped Caribola Resort. With its secluded and rocky beach nestled between two verdant mountains, it reminded me of an upscale Hawaiian resort. Staff at the resort entrance gate dissuaded us from hiking the slippery tide pools trail because Carol lacked proper hiking shoes. Instead, we hitched a ride back to Cane Beach, from a couple we met on our Buck Island tour. Dinner at Eat@Cane Bay restaurant consisted of fresh brownies and ice cream. As we awaited our taxi ride back to Christiansted, we watched several women riding horses through the sunset-lit surf.

To learn more about St. Croix's culture, history, botany, and rum, we went sightseeing with a native Cruzan, Mr. Sweeny, of St. Croix Safari Tours. St. Croix has a year-round population of almost sixty thousand, including four thousand former New York wage slaves. There are 150 churches on the island. The oldest is a Lutheran church in Christiansted called Steeple Church. St. Croix has a government consisting of a governor, fifty state senators and, one US congressman. As a US territory, it has no vote in the US Congress, but its three electoral votes help elect the president. Besides its politicians, St. Croix has celebrity basketball leaders like Tim Duncan of the San Antonio Spurs and Raja Bell, who plays for the Utah Jazz. Their murals adorn the walls of a popular Christiansted restaurant.

Old-growth mahogany trees lined the road as we left the city for the countryside. Going west on Route 70, we passed the impressive University of the Virgin Islands campus, established in 1962, and the Vocational Tech Center. Small roadside stands sold fresh lobster and fish. Goat farms dotted the hillsides, and every President's Day, twenty to thirty thousand people attend the island's agricultural fair.

Depending on your gender preference, we rode on the Kings/Queens Highway by a Catholic high school on the way to St. George Village Botanical Gardens. Because it's an island, St. Croix has few indigenous plants and trees. Their botanical garden conserves and preserves living collections of over fifteen hundred native and exotic species, including some from Brazil and India. The oddest looking trees, like the Cannonball and Sausage, had names that accurately described the shape and size of their seed pods. The painkiller tree had a white prickly seed that oozed a pungent smelling jelly used to relieve pain and swelling. The ylang-ylang tree produced yellowish-green leaves that make Chanel perfume.

Like a corner drugstore, the gardens included over fifty medicinal herbs. Because sugarcane plantations lacked doctors, weed women, knowledgeable about healing herbs, treated plantation owner and slave families. While bush doctors embellished their remedies with astrological lore, most St. Croix herbalists successfully treated headaches, insomnia, gonorrhea, and diarrhea with proven herbal remedies.

Rum is to the Virgin Islands as tequila is to Mexico. So we toured the Cruzan Rum Factory to learn how rum is made. A twenty-one-year-old male, wearing dreadlocks, Cruzan Rum T-shirt, baggy shorts, and white running shoes, guided us through the still house and warehouse. Cruzan workers first mixed water, molasses, and yeast in heated fermentation tanks to produce a mixture of 10 percent alcohol and 90 percent waste. Second, five stainless steel and copper stills separated headache-producing impurities (fusil oils and heads) from the alcohol. Third, waste workers treated liquid waste and piped it into the ocean while they sent solid waste to the landfill or sold it as fertilizer. Fourth, workers filled oak barrels with rum distillate and aged it in the warehouse for two to twelve years. During the aging process, as much as half the rum evaporated and became "the angel's share." Finally, tanker trucks delivered the rum to Jim Beam's bottling and flavoring plant in Florida. As sugar magically changed to rum before our eyes, our guide transformed into a bartender and served us Mango Tangos in the tasting room.

Our next tour stop was Frederiksted, also known as Freedom City. Governor General Peter von Scholten signed the proclamation freeing St. Croix slaves there in 1848. Like Christiansted, Frederiksted is a waterfront town and the second largest town on St. Croix. Victorian-style buildings replaced the town's original buildings destroyed by fire in 1758.

We stopped for lunch at a restaurant next to Frederiksted's cruise ship terminal. I munched on a sandwich in sight of six brown pelicans roosting on a moored speedboat. I jokingly said the pelicans must be discussing the *Pelican Brief* movie. A fellow traveler, who I assumed spoke "pelicanese," said actually, "They were talking about the merits of boxers versus briefs."

After the Danes bought St. Croix from the French, they established three hundred sugarcane plantations. The Whim Plantation House and Museum we visited was a typical eighteenth-century example. Ninety of its 150 acres was devoted to sugarcane and rum production. One 1754 museum document listed the names, ages, occupations, and birthplaces of the plantation's slaves. The restored great house, museum, windmill, and plantation buildings featured antiques, photos, tools, sugar-processing equipment, and historical records. St Croix's last sugarcane plantation closed in the 1960s, when it became cheaper to make molasses from sugar beets.

Whim Plantation Windmill

Highly labor intensive, sugarcane production relied on inexpensive slave labor to make it profitable. After planting sugarcane root stock in holes, between thirteen and sixteen months passed before it could be harvested. One gang cut down the cane and bundled it on carts. The carts took the crop to the mill, where another gang fed it into rollers that squeezed out the sugary juice piped to the boiling house. Crushed cane called *baggar* was used as animal feed or fuel. The boiling house's copper kettles boiled the sugarcane juice and sent it to the distillery to separate the molasses from the rum. The process continued twenty-four hours a day at the height of West Indies' rum production.

Like most buildings on St. Croix, workers built the Whim Plantation great house with limestone and crushed coral, using molasses as mortar. Danish builders used ship ballast bricks to build fireplaces and stoves. Island mahogany was used for flooring and furniture on display in the ball room, living room, and master bedroom. An eight-foot-deep stone moat surrounded the plantation house.

On the road back to Christiansted, we traveled through St. Croix's only rain forest. It was six miles long and one-quarter mile wide. In 1989, Hurricane Hugo destroyed 30 percent of its trees, with 250 mile-per-hour winds. A licorice tree, felled by the storm, lie alongside the road with new life sprouting from it. During the hurricane, our guide and his family huddled in their house under a queen-sized mattress until their roof blew off. The winds carried the roof for a mile. I have never experienced a hurricane, but three of my brothers survived Hurricane Charley, when its 150 mile-per-hour winds battered southwest Florida in 2004.

The forecast called for clouds and beer as we stopped at the Mt.Pellier Hut Domino Club bar and restaurant to see its beer-drinking pigs. Legend has it that the popular bar and restaurant started as a small hole-in-the-jungle bamboo rum shack with one stand up table shaded by a grass umbrella. One day a pig wandered into the watering hole and thirsty patrons shared their beer with him. The pig became a regular and locals nicknamed him Buster. Word spread about the beer swilling swine attracting increased business. As a result, the bar expanded and added a restaurant. Unfortunately, Buster and his liver succumbed to cirrhosis. Buried behind the bar, a memorial with his picture and empty beer cans mark his grave. Two popular porcine take his place in wooden stalls next to the bar and restaurant. Due to Humane Society complaints, these porkers only partake of nonalcoholic suds. A professional film crew hogged the pig's attention, taping what I assumed to be an O'Doul's beer commercial or You-tube video before it was our turn to toast. I placed a can of O'Doul's (shaken, not stirred) between tooth and snout and got showered in flying suds. The smell of urine was so bad it reminded me of the book *Yellow River* by I. P. Freely.

Pickled Porker

Leaving the rain forest, we passed a cattle farm that reminded me of the Parker Ranch in Hawaii. This five-hundred-acre farm was located next to St. Croix's highest point, Mt. Eagle. Athletes training for Hawaii's annual Ironman Triathlon cycle along steep and winding Carousel Road nicknamed "The Beast."

To explore the east side of St. Croix Island, we rented a car. We briefly stopped at Cramer Beach, a local hangout with picnic tables and restrooms. Across the street, we looked at the Baseline Array telescope from outside a chain linked fence. Astronomers and geoscientists use it to study space, and it was featured in Jodie Foster's movie, *Contact.*

Before reaching the easternmost part of the United States (Point Udall), we explored a picturesque beach bordered by organ pipe cactus, frangipani trees, and bromeliads. Carol collected small rose-colored shells and polished green glass pieces for her fused glass business. A US Customs airport agent kindly let us keep the souvenirs, despite Homeland Security regulations prohibiting it.

Compared to our vacations on St. John and St. Thomas, Carol and I enjoyed St. Croix the best. Our bed and breakfast was first-rate, restaurants and tours great, and the people friendly. Our condominium and food on St. Thomas were excellent, but Amalie Harbor lacked the charm of Christiansted, especially when cruise ships docked. Our accommodation in St. John's Cruz Bay was one step above camping, and the weather was fair at best. Honeymoon Beach was awesome, and we never felt crowded by other tourists.

Overall, we found Cruzans, especially our hosts, to be welcoming with good senses of humor. Although renting a car was a hassle, once we did, we learned how polite drivers were. Instead of honking their horns in anger or frustration, they used a short beep to say hi and a longer one to say thank you if you drove courteously. Every Friday night in Christiansted, locals, tourists, food vendors, and merchants filled downtown streets and sidewalks for Jump Night. Live steel drum music filled the air, as *moko jumbies* (costumed stilt walkers) shook hands with bystanders for dollar bills.

Chapter Twelve

New Mexico and New Grandson Memories

The first time I read the word *ecotone*, I was on an April 2010 New Mexico road trip with my son Christopher. We agreed it would make a great name for an indie band. Reading a display sign in Bandelier National Monument, we learned that ecotones were places where species from different habitats coexist. Like species from different habitats we joined visitors from other states and countries to learn about a civilization that lived in adobe (mud, wood, and rock) houses attached to caves built on the side of a mountain.

Five ancient Puebloan groups (Chaco, Mesa Verde, Little Colorado, Kayentu, and Rio Grande) lived in the four corners of the United States from 100 BC to AD 1600. Although the groups represented different tribes, they shared many skills like farming, weaving, and pottery making.

Ten thousand years ago, ancestors of present-day Pueblo residents moved in and out of the Parajarito Plateau, pursuing large game animals. Twenty five hundred years later, a drier and warmer climate caused glaciers to recede, killing large game animals. As a result, hunters killed smaller animals and collected edible plants for food. Around 500 BC, the Northern Rio Grande Valley's population increased, as roving Puebloan tribes built permanent adobe homes. Later, the tribes built homes with stone blocks, plastered together with mud. We saw ruins of these homes at the Pecos National Historical Park.

Around AD 325, the Frijoles Canyon Puebloan population peaked at seven hundred, with one village in Bandelier National Park, housing approximately one hundred people in four hundred rooms. Long House was eight hundred feet of adjoining, multistoried stone homes with hand-carved caves as back rooms. Exploring these caves, I felt like a bat flitting through dimly lit spaces, which appeared as Swiss cheese–like holes from a distance.

It is not hard to understand why ancient tribes from Utah, Arizona, Colorado, and New Mexico established a large permanent settlement at Bandelier. Like the animals they hunted, tribes needed to live near year-round water, and the Frijoles River seemed a natural choice. They also needed the shelter and security offerred by the mountains and cottonwood trees that lined the river canyon. Yucca plants provided fibers for sandals, baskets, and rope while ponderosa pines provided house ceiling beams called *vigas*.

Different peoples peacefully coexisted, because they shared common spiritual and cultural beliefs. An underground structure, called a kiva, was the center of their community, not only for religious purposes, but also for education and decision making. Like the yucca fiber that held their baskets together, religious beliefs were the threads that bound many families. Elders passed down knowledge and faith to children within the kiva, much like other ancestral communities.

Art reflected Puebloan trading, building, and ceremonial practices. For example, one petroglyph of a macaw symbolized what inhabitants obtained from Mexican traders in exchange for obsidian tools. Another petroglyph depicting a basalt axe showed a tool used or traded by the Puebloans. Finally, a petroglyph of a turkey honored an animal prized for its ceremonial feathers and edible meat.

Certain construction techniques used in Bandelier suggest knowledge brought to the area by distant tribal members. Monument remains of irrigation canals, water gardens, and terraces indicated widespread control of imported water and soil conservation techniques.

Our family of young and old couples, families with small children, single men and women, moved through the ruins like ancient Puebloans. Hiking along the park's four-mile main loop trail, we walked in dirt through pine forests, under the gaze of mule deer. We climbed wooden ladders 140 feet high to ceremonial kivas carved into stone alcoves. I connected with another climber, when I remarked that it was the seven-thousand-foot altitude, rather than lack of fitness that caused us to breathe so heavily. Perched high in eroded tuff walls, we sat like swallows, resting before flight. Parents taught children, strangers shared stories, and photographers memorialized sacred ground with digital rather than stone petroglyphs.

Hungry from our high-altitude hike, Christopher and I ate lunch at the park's visitor center snack bar. I had leftover Mexican food and oatmeal cookies while Christopher ordered a burrito from the cafe menu. We reflected on the second day of our New Mexico road trip, shared with global villagers, and how the experience deepened our understanding of ecotones. A word primarily used to describe how animal species adapt to each other and their differing habitats now was a metaphor for peaceful coexistence among humans, living and interacting in a more connected global society.

To further understand how art connects villagers in our global society, we explored the indoor and outdoor art galleries in Santa Fe. The fictional account that follows was inspired by our daylong art walk.

From the fountain of life emerged a marine creature of extraordinary features. She floated on a black marble surface, gazing into a spiral shell. Her upper torso was raised in a cobra pose, and on her head, she wore white jagged coral. Her lower body ended with the upward extended tail of a gray whale.

This green sea siren seemed misplaced in the high desert on a narrow canyon road. Mermaids belonged in the sea, not in an arid region that endured nine drought years. Maybe she drew energy from the koi swimming around the base of her rock pedestal. Or was it the spiritual richness of desert soil that germinated religious thought?

To answer this riddle, father and son asked the wise koi. They replied, "You must visit a Mediterranean goddess, who has knowledge from the Far East." So we continued down the canyon road and stopped at a Buddhist temple. Entering the temple, an olive-complexioned face and smile, framed in brown curls, greeted us. We asked her how the mermaid survived in the desert. She pointed toward a painting of a porcelain-skinned Chinese girl adorning the temple wall. We learned that birds and butterflies, symbolizing beauty and freedom, had helped her overcome years of oppression.

Exiting the temple, green sea turtle and frog sculptures beckoned us from a stony outcropping. They too had lived without water in the desert, like the mysterious sea maiden. We asked them, "How can you live so far from water"? They answered, "We don't know, ask the birds."

A red and green gallery appeared on our left. The gallery's door opened, like a drawbridge. Walking over a moat, we entered the gallery and saw sandhill cranes perched from wall sconces. They told us about their recent trip to an ocean estuary in Bosque del Apache National Park.

Down the narrowing canyon like a flash flood, we rushed to a circular building that looked like a yurt. Through glass doors, we entered a high-ceilinged room with nothing on its walls but a large rectangular painting.

Dark blues of deep water, light blues of windswept waves, and greenish-blues of shallow water splashed off the canvas, like foamy ocean spray. We smelled the briny water and felt its warm caress on our ankles as we waded forward through bubbling sand.

Immersed in crystal clear saltwater, we opened our eyes and surprisingly could see marine life clearly without prescription snorkeling masks. We swam underwater without needing oxygen tanks and followed a trail marked by elkhorn, staghorn, and brain corals. Currents powered by sea fans propelled us forward, through schools of tropical fish.

A sea cave shaped like an enormous conch shell loomed before us. We swam through the cave's pink and white opening into dark creases and crevices that spiraled deeper into the ocean floor. Despite the darkness, we saw without headlamps. Black granite fish heads, planted in the sand like ancient totems, quietly hummed a sea shanty. The sound got louder and lower as we tunneled inward.

Suddenly, black dolphins surrounded us and grabbed our outstretched hands with their fins. We clasped the fins tightly and held on for dear life. As our bodies were launched upward through corridors of sand and shell, our ears no longer heard the bass hum of a sea shanty. Instead, we heard high-pitched laughter as the sea pressure changed. Sand blasted our faces as we accelerated toward the surface.

Father and son, towed by marine mammals, emerged from their dark, cold, and watery tomb into bright, warm sunshine that wrapped around their bodies like a Puebloan blanket. Sitting on two stone fish heads in a gravel courtyard, we saw ten other trout sculptures surrounding us. Their arched bodies cast shadows on the glistening gravel. The shadows spelled out the answer to our riddle—*imagination.*

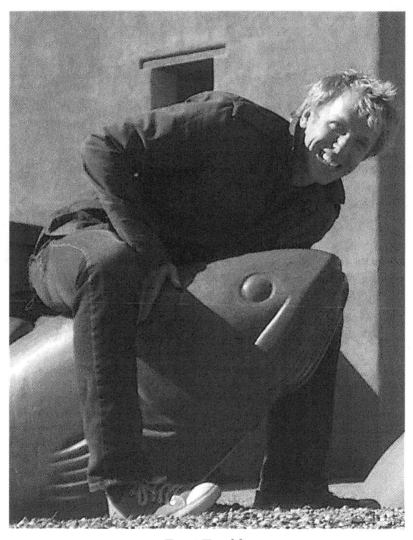

Trout Trouble

From tales about water, we turned our attention to the power of fire and wind. Volcanic eruptions from several Cascade Mountains shaped Washington, Oregon, and Idaho topography. Much the same happened in New Mexico, where we explored two important volcanic blast zones that shaped its landscape.

Fiery magma and cooled ash bursting from volcanic vents sculpted the desert lands of the Southwest, especially New Mexico. Eruptions six hundred times more powerful than the 1980 Mount St. Helens' blast covered four hundred square miles with a blanket of volcanic ash up to one thousand feet thick. But rather than lull the land to sleep, wind, fog, and rain chiseled ash-hardened cinders into cones, mesas, plateaus, prairies, and calderas. In *Rising From the Plains*, John McPhee writes about the power of wind in shaping high country geology in Wyoming:

> "Now looking from mountains to mountains along the Laramie Plains—his gaze bridging fifty miles of what had recently been solid ground—Love said he thought the role of the wind had been much greater than hitherto suspected in the Exhumation of the Rockies . . . We know however, the approximate volume of sediment from the Powder River Basin, the Bighorn Basin, the Wind River Basin, the Laramie Basin, and so forth. We can say it all went down to the Mississippi Delta . . . Streams only account for about half the material . . . Since it's not all in the delta, where did it go? I think the wind took it".

Capulin Volcano was one of the landforms resulting from New Mexico's explosive past. Southeast of the New Mexico/Colorado border, Interstate 25 took Christopher and I to Capulin's cinder cone, which rose over thirteen hundred feet above the surrounding plains. Unlike lava cones in eastern Oregon, Capulin's slopes were full of varied and abundant vegetation. Prairie grasses, pinyon juniper, and ponderosa pine dotted the base and cone with a green-and-brown glaze hardened by kilnlike temperatures.

We drove to another New Mexico geologic feature, Valles Caldera, near Los Alamos, known more for man-made explosive events. Covered in snow, this fifteen-mile-wide crater looked like a wider and shallower version of Crater Lake, Oregon and a lot bigger than Crater Lake in Colorado. It formed 1.2 million years ago, when the center of the Jemez volcanic field erupted, spewing soft volcanic tuff. Ancient Puebloans used tuff that resembled limestone to build homes. Others have compared Valles Caldera to the crater left by the detonation of America's first atomic bomb.

When New Mexico native Jim Morrison sang "Light My Fire," I wondered if he got his inspiration from the state's smoldering history. Red hot cinders and ash shape-shifted into mysterious and magical forms. Fire continues to impact the state's landscape. Natural-caused fires in 1977 and 1996 burned almost 40 percent of Bandelier National Monument's trees and plants. In 2000, a park service prescribed fire burned along mountain slopes and through residential Los Alamos neighborhoods. As a Tewa resident of Taos Pueblo said, "Yea, that one got away from them."

During our road trip northwest of Santa Fe, Christopher and I drove on State Route 4 from Bandelier National Monument past Valles Caldera and through Jemez Pueblo lands. On a current New Mexico's Department of Transportation Map, State Route 4 is marked by a blue line like all of the old back roads were on historic highway maps of America. William Least Heat-Moon's evocative description of these old roads chronicled in *Blue Highways* seemed applicable:

> "But in those brevities just before dawn and a little after dusk-times neither dark nor night-the old roads return to the sky some of its color. Then, in truth, they carry a mysterious cast of blue, and it's that time when the pull of the blue highway is strongest, when the open road is a beckoning, a strangeness, a place where a man can lose himself."

Blue Highway, Red Rocks

From Bandelier's ancient ruins, the highway passed through pine forests and red rock tribal lands. Smoke from a prescribed burn filled the forest air. Hazy skies turned clear blue as we drove west. Fiery red rocks mesmerized us and made me stop the car and admire the beauty of Jemez Pueblo. Soft, puffy white clouds dotted the azure sky and contrasted with the prickly thorns of yellow, green, and red cactus. Christopher snapped a digital photo of the awe-inspiring scenery and sent it by cell phone to his roommate in Brooklyn, New York. His roommate could not believe it was a photograph. He thought it was a painting.

Our New Mexico road trip finished, Christopher and I returned to Aurora, Colorado, to rejoin Carol, Rachel, Phil, and my new grandson, Sampson. The tranquil calm of our road trip quickly dissolved as the robust cry of a hungry six-week old infant created instant tension. Not until I held Sampson in my arms for the first time to feed him his bottle did the serenity of blue highways return. After giving him a small bottle of milk, I successfully burped him over my left shoulder. As he relaxed in my arms, I cradled his head on my left arm while my right arm supported the rest of his tiny body. I enjoyed almost every sound, facial expression, and body twitch of this special gift from God as I lulled him to sleep in a rocking chair. Stroking his soft head and wispy dark hair, caressing his cheeks and gazing into his eyes reawakened nurturing feelings dormant since Rachel and Christopher were infants.

Bonding with my son during our New Mexico road trip to Santa Fe, Bandelier National Park and Pecos National Historical Park brought us closer together through our mutual love of nature, writing and the visual arts. My visit to see Rachel, Phil and baby Sampson increased my pride for my daughter, son-in-law and new grandson. I looked forward to sharing future travel experiences with my extended family.

Conclusion

As Mark Twain wrote in *Innocents Abroad*, "Broad, wholesome, and charitable views of men and things cannot be acquired by vegetating in one little corner of the earth all one's lifetime." From the cocoon of fraternity life at an elite American university, I broadened my wings to taste art's nectar aged in Western European capital cities, cathedrals, museums, and bucolic countrysides. Emboldened by a two-month cycling odyssey, I gained confidence and strength and learned the value of love and perseverance.

Toughened and challenged by Alaska's rugged landscape, I learned to survive long dark winter days and to feed a family of four from fish caught in the state's bountiful rivers and ocean waters. I gained respect for the land and its subsistence culture practiced by both Alaskan sourdoughs and Native Americans.

A cruise to Nova Scotia and St. John, Canada, reinforced my admiration for our northern neighbors, who share many of the qualities found in people of the Last Frontier.

Winter getaways to the US Virgin Islands warmed my heart and soul and opened my eyes to the injustices of the African slave trade. Mexican grottoes reminded me of the global reach of Christianity while Costa Rica raised my awareness of immigration issues and the healing powers of peaceful coexistence.

Touring East Coast American cities, two decades after moving west, renewed my interest in US history and how both coasts are connected by the pioneering and comedic spirit of midwesterners. My travels both in the US and abroad made me see and feel how nature, geology and geography connects us all in a global ecotone that depends upon clean oceans and rivers, sustainable forests, clear mountain views and an undying conservation ethic in all.

For those not inspired to leave your little corner of the world, I hope what you read here about new places and faces will calm your fears, fill your heart, and enrich your soul. If reading is boring, tiring, or not an option, then listen to books about different settings and cultures. Explore audio books that open your mind and expand your dreamscape. Mark Twain's views ring true today, 150 years after he wrote them: "Travel is fatal to prejudice, bigotry, and narrow-mindedness, and many of our people need it sorely on these accounts." Exposure to new locales, languages and lifestyles taught me lessons beyond the classroom which helped me understand who I was and the path I should take to become a self-fulfilled individual

About the Author

An award winning nature photographer and writer, Mr. Bresky earned an undergraduate minor in English at the University of Pennsylvania. Most recently he completed his training to be a volunteer naturalist in metropolitan Portland, Oregon. After receiving a masters degree in public administration he cowrote journalistic-type reports published by the US General Accounting/Accountability Office (GAO) for twenty-seven years and traveled extensively in the United States. He researched environmental issues, interviewed federal, state and local experts and reported on natural resource issues including parks, forests and fish and wildllife management. His reports influenced executive and legislative branch leaders on both sides of the political aisle. After retiring from federal service and earning his teaching certificate from Portland State University, he taught in Oregon public schools for nine years. As a self-employed writer and photographer, he continues to take workshops on writing and photography and is an active volunteer in the Three Rivers Artists Guild in Oregon City, Oregon.